Democratizing Cleveland

Democratizing Cleveland

The Rise and Fall of Community Organizing
in
Cleveland, Ohio 1975-1985

by Randy Cunningham

Arambala Press
Cleveland, Ohio

Requests for permission to reprint or to make copies, and for any
other information, should be addressed to the publisher:

Arambala Press
P.O. Box 14268
Cleveland, Ohio 44114
info@arambalapress.com
www.arambalapress.com

ISBN 978-0-9797206-0-4

Printed in Cleveland, Ohio by Orange Blossom Press
1935 West 25th St.
Cleveland, Ohio 44113

Cover photo by Maria A. Schaefer. Permission granted by the
Cleveland Press Archives, University Library, Cleveland State University.

I hear sometimes people talking about how the police need to do, how the councilmen needs to do, how the mayor or governor or some other official needs to do. There was a sense that we need to do, and I think that that's what organizing ... helps people to recognize because there's something that we need to do.

– Hugh Kidd, *Union Miles*

Table of Contents

Preface

In 1980 I moved to Cleveland to go to graduate school. I soon decided that academia was not for me and I left my program. I got a job with a neighborhood non-profit housing corporation called the Near West Housing Corporation. The corporation was a spinoff of Near West Neighbors in Action.

Working for Near West Housing pitched me into the middle of the ferment of the community organizing movement in Cleveland. Today in Cleveland, neighborhood organizations describe themselves as an "industry", or a "sector" of the economy, little different from a normal business or corporation. When I started in 1981, we consciously described ourselves as a "movement".

We operated as a ready reserve for our mother community organization. I attended block club meetings, helped Near West Neighbors in Action prepare for conventions, leafleted neighborhoods, and participated in actions, or "hits" as they were called. Two of the actions I took part in, the SOHIO stockholders hit, and the Hunt Club hit, were two of the more infamous actions of the community organizations of Cleveland, and two of the most important in determining the fate of the movement. I always thought that there were good stories waiting to be told about this movement. Telling those stories was the goal of mine in writing this history.

This is the first history of community organizing in Cleveland. I hope it is not the last, and I look forward to it being surpassed. Cleveland has a fascinating social movement history, the surface of which has not even been scratched. There are many stories to tell, and I hope others will join in telling them.

Acknowledgments

It is hoped that this history of community organizing will return to the community at least a fraction of what I have gained from working in Cleveland's neighborhoods. It could not have been written without the interest and cooperation of the veterans of this era of community organizing. I hope they find that it does the period justice.

I want to start by acknowledging the invaluable help of the staff of the Archives of the Catholic Diocese of Cleveland and the Archives of the Western Reserve Historical Society. In particular, I wish to single out Chris Krosel of the Catholic Diocese of Cleveland for her help with finding documents and for sharing her knowledge of many of the topics and events covered in this history. A special thanks goes to Lynn M. Duchez Bycko, Special Collections Associate of the Cleveland State University Library, for helping me hunt down the front cover photograph for this book.

A number of people read the manuscript in part or in its entirety through its many drafts. They insured that I did not leave the field of non-fiction. They are Dr. Robert Kleidman, Cleveland State University; Dr. Dennis Keating, Cleveland State University; Dr. Randy Stoecker, University of Toledo; Dr. Robert Fisher, University of Connecticut; Dr. Todd Swanstrom, St. Louis University. Additional readers were Bill Callahan, Tom Gannon, Joe Mariano, Charles Murray, Chris Krosel, Rev. Bob Begin, Kate McGuiness, and Frank Ford. I want to especially thank Tom Gannon and Frank Ford. Tom showed an early interest in the project, read drafts, and was always available to answer any questions I may have had. Frank provided a meticulous reading of one of the final drafts of the manuscript. The product benefited greatly from the breadth and depth of his knowledge of Cleveland, its neighborhoods, and its community organizations. We also love to talk about this subject, and I benefited as much from these freewheeling conversations as I did from the actual written comments.

Frank, along with Kenia Colon of Neighborhood Progress, Inc., helped organize a committee made up of experienced neighborhood activists and veterans of the events described in this book who reviewed the manuscript and provided invaluable help and suggestions in its development and editing. The committee members were Frank Ford, Kenia Colon, Larry Bresler, Phil Star, Norm Krumholz, Tom Gannon, Inez Killingsworth, Joe Garcia, Mark Seifert, Rob Kleidman, and Linda Hudecek. Thanks to my copy editor Pat Fernberg for straightening out the mess I gave her.

I want to thank Dr. Robert Kleidman for his help in writing a grant to the Aspen Institute, and the cigars we smoked when it was awarded. I especially want to thank the Aspen Institute for its support, which made it possible to transcribe the interviews for the project.

It is now time to acknowledge the people who really made this book possible: those whom I interviewed. They are Larry Allen, Gloria Aron, Chuck Ackerman, Thomas Andrzejewski, George Barany, Mabelee Barker, Rev. Bob Begin, Dan Berry, Rene Berry, Paul Buccino, Sharon Bryant, Len Calabrese, Bill Callahan, John Calkins, Pat Carney, Janice Cogger, Lana Cowell, Leola Criswell, Peggy Croftcheck, Neil Conway, Alma Cooper, Pitt Curtiss, Henry Doll, Fran Dostal, Ted Dostal, Kate Monter Durban, Ken Esposito, Harry Fagan, Frank Ford, Tom Gannon, Joe Garcia, Holly Gigante, Ramona Golden, Denise Gordeev, Bill Gruber, Norm Harrison, David Hoehnen, Linda Hudecek, Kathy Jaksic, Ron Jaksic, Helen Jones, Ken Jones, Marita Kavalec, Eileen Kelly, Hugh Kidd, Inez Killingsworth, Pat Kinney, Sandra Kluk, Ken Kovach, Bernice Krumhansl, Norm Krumholz, David Leighton, Vince Lombardi, Gail Long, Mark McDermott, Sharon McGraw, Kate McGuiness, Charles Murray, Barbara Nagy, Karen Nielson, Michael O'Brien, Ruth Ann O'Leary, Judi Opalach, Barb Pertz, Bob Pollack, Ann Pratt, Bobbi Reichtell, Dan Reidy, Joanne Roberts, Helen Knipe Smith, Phil Star, Melinda Smythe, Lenny Strimpel, Pearl Toth, Sarah Turner, Shel Trapp, Wesley Walker, Thomas Wagner, Charlotte Wells, Marlene Weslian, Doug Van Auken, Diane Yambor, Dorothy Zeigler.

I want to give special attention to the interviews of Harry Fagan. Harry Fagan was dying of cancer when I was starting my research. I spoke to him briefly, but he was too sick to be interviewed. He did give me a lead on finding a series of interviews that were conducted by Earl Landau in 1983 before Fagan left Cleveland. I was able to contact Earl Landau, and he sent me what I consider a set of tapes worth their weight in gold. The day I picked those tapes up at the post office was one of the high points of the process of writing this book. Thank you, Earl. If it weren't for you and your generosity, this history would have had a huge hole in it. Many thanks to you.

Finally, I want to thank my wife, Tristine Michelle Roberts, for insisting that I was a writer long before I believed it myself.

Introduction

For a decade between the mid-1970s and 1980s, the neighborhoods of Cleveland, Ohio hosted a vibrant community organizing movement. This movement put a pro-neighborhood agenda on center stage in a city that was the very definition of the term "urban crisis".

During the previous decade of the 1960s, Cleveland witnessed persistent racial conflict, two major riots, the devastation and development of urban renewal, and political reform and change as represented by the administration of Carl B. Stokes, the first African-American mayor of a major U.S. city. As Cleveland entered the 1970s, it faced not only the unresolved problems of the previous decade, but new challenges, as well, such as massive deindustrialization. Compounding this disaster were the poisonous politics of Cleveland City Hall, the redlining of the city by financial institutions and insurance companies, white flight, and the departure of the city's middle class to the suburbs.

Throughout this period, Cleveland's neighborhoods were either ignored or were subjected to the tender mercies of financial institutions, corporations, politicians, planners, and bureaucracies from city hall to Washington. What the poor and working class residents of Cleveland's neighborhoods lacked was a way to address their own problems with their own solutions and to challenge their status as pawns in the games of others.

Starting in the early 1970s, activists who had been inspired and educated in the civil rights and anti-war movements began to search for a grassroots response to the failures of elite initiatives to solve the problems of the city's neighborhoods. The result of their efforts was a grassroots movement that fought disinvestment and redlining from financial institutions and insurance companies, demanded democratic accountability and fairness in the delivery of city services and government programs, and required that development serve the neighborhoods, not just downtown Cleveland.

Throughout the city, this movement built neighborhood-based community organizations representing hundreds of block clubs. Their conventions were attended by thousands of neighborhood residents. They helped train ordinary Clevelanders in the skills of organization and democratic life. The movement won significant concessions from Cleveland's powerful financial institutions which began reinvesting in the neighborhoods. Government bureaucracies were taught new lessons in accountability by the people they had always ignored or dismissed. Politicians had their worlds turned upside down.

Within a decade of the start of this movement, it was over. Few organizations survived the mid-1980s, and those that did were either pale shadows of their former selves or were very different organizations with very different agendas, where only the name on the letterhead remained the same. The initiative shifted from the grassroots back to the traditional powers that have always ruled Cleveland under the banner of development as represented by non-profit community development corporations. The catch was that development was not democracy. No one was so rude to say that in the glare of groundbreakings, leveraged deals, and the rise of a new neighborhood-based development bureaucracy. Flannel shirts, placards, and sit-ins at bank headquarters were out, and suits and spreadsheets were in.

The community organizations of Cleveland perished because they could not adapt to major changes in their environment. These changes included the presidency of Ronald Reagan and the rise of conservatism, the departure of key supporters in the Catholic Diocese of Cleveland, the change in the leadership of the diocese, and a shift in foundation interest from the always-problematic world of organizing to the much safer world of development. An even more important reason for their demise was that the traditional power brokers of Cleveland regained their footing after the chaos of the 1960s and the challenge of the Kucinich administration and reasserted their power and their command of the decision-making process in the city. This decision-making process had no room for the rough-and-ready school of grassroots democracy championed by the old community organizations.

This book is dedicated to those who continue to pursue the vision of a just and democratic Cleveland. I hope it provides them with something useful for their future work.

Part 1:

The Origins of Community Organizing in Cleveland

Chapter 1

CLEVELAND: YOU GOTTA BE TOUGH

Cleveland, Ohio, in the late nineteenth and early twentieth centuries was an industrial boom town with a reputation as one of the most progressive, well run cities in the nation. Its character was established by its civic and business leaders and by an ethnically and racially diverse population that had been drawn to the city by employment opportunities in its industries.

Cleveland had all the assets and all the liabilities common to the industrial cities of the Gilded Age. Its liabilities included great inequalities of wealth and power, the inequities of the shop floor, poverty, poor housing, racial strife, and breathtaking environmental destruction.

The period after World War II brought a new list of burdens and problems for the city. Few cities were more ravaged by urban renewal than Cleveland was. The interstate highway system became a death warrant for America's older cities, and it slashed through urban neighborhoods and gave birth to a suburban regime of endless sprawl that drained both population and wealth from cities like Cleveland. These burdens were exacerbated by one of the greatest body blows ever delivered to a city built on industry: the deindustrialization of America.

Cleveland industries were based on transportation, the iron and steel industries, petroleum and chemicals, garments, electrical products, and automobiles. In 1930, at the zenith of its growth, Cleveland was second only to Detroit in the percentage of its workforce employed in industry. The Cleveland metropolitan region was rated eighth in the country in the number of industrial employees and seventh in value of its products in 1931. The 1930s saw the stagnation of Cleveland industry. The U.S. census of 1954 showed no essential change in its industrial makeup from the past. That stagnation continued into the 1970s and 1980s. The industrial job loss between 1979 and 1986 was devastating. By 1986, only twenty nine per cent of the total employment in the Cleveland metropolitan area was industrial. Cleveland had lost thirty per cent of its manufacturing employment.[1]

The industrial decline of Cleveland was matched by a decline in the population of the city. In 1950, the city reached its highest population: 914,808. In 1960, the population was 876,050. Losses reported by the U.S. Census Bureau between 1970 and 1980 show in dramatic detail the decline of the city. In 1970, the population was 750,879. By 1980, it was 573,822, a loss of 177,057 residents. No ten-year period before or since has witnessed a freefall in population comparable to that of the 1970s.[2]

The 1960s were dominated by the politics of racial conflict. Cleveland had been a hotbed of abolitionist sentiment in the period before and during the Civil War. It continued to have an enlightened racial atmosphere, even as the rest of the nation buried the hatchet of the Civil War in the backs of former slaves. African-Americans in Cleveland enjoyed progress and employment in a wide range of occupations.

This reputation, along with Cleveland's burgeoning industries, made it a major destination for the northern migration of African-Americans from the south known as The Great Migration. At the time of World War I, 10,000 African-Americans made their homes in Cleveland. By 1930, that population had increased to 72,000.[3]

While conditions in Cleveland were much better than in the south, what the new African-American residents found was far from the promised land that the propaganda about Cleveland portrayed. As Cleveland became an industrial boom town the city assembled an industrial workforce of immigrants from Europe who soon learned racism along with English. This new population competed with the established African-American population for jobs, housing, status, and political power. Discrimination that had heretofore been rare became more common.[4] This collision between myth and reality laid the foundations for civil rights activism after World War II, and the political rise of a true son of the Great Migration, Carl Stokes.

It also led to a collision between the white ethnic population of Cleveland that had a vested interest in maintaining the racial status quo and an African-American population determined to destroy that status quo. The conflict was fought in all the arenas where the promise of Cleveland had been denied to those who had come to the city with so much hope. It also resulted in one of two riots in Cleveland in the 1960s.

The Hough riot, that stretched from July 18 to 24, 1966 began when a white tavern in Hough put up a sign, "No Water for Niggers". A crowd gathered outside the club, the police were called, and the riot was on. By the time it was over, four African-Americans were dead, hundreds were injured, and in jail, and property damage ranged from $1 million to $2 million. The city establishment was in shock, dumbfounded at the reasons for the riot. The African-American community answered because it had been ignored.[5] They responded to being ignored not only by rioting, but by sparking the drive to elect Carl Stokes as the first African-American mayor of a major U.S. city. That dream came true in 1967.

At first, Stokes enjoyed the support of the business community, but this did not last once they realized that he was serious about helping his community and was not just a provider of riot insurance. He ran afoul of class divisions in the African-American community. He had to deal with the twin curses of all Cleveland mayors: a police department that does not recognize civilian authority and a city council that had no use for mayoral power, especially a mayor who was the sworn enemy of the racial status quo.

The beginning of the end for Stokes was the 1968 Glenville shootout, when black militant Fred Ahmed Evans staged a showdown with the Cleveland police. The result was a riot that lasted from July 23 to 28 in which seven people were killed and more than $2 million in property was damaged. The National Guard was called in. In one of his most controversial moves, Stokes withdrew all white police from the area and replaced them with African-American police officers and community leaders. Most damaging of all was the discovery that the guns Evans used for his confrontation had been purchased with money from one of the administration's community programs. Stokes's corporate backers ran for cover and abandoned him.[6]

The remainder of Stokes's tenure in office was a running battle with the African-American elite, the Cleveland police department, and a hostile city council. It was also marred by blunders by the mayor, such as the disastrous appointment of General Benjamin O. Davis to head the police department. Stokes did not run again for office in 1972. It was not until 1989, with the election of Michael R. White, that another African-American occupied the mayor's office. In spite of what appeared to have been a failed administration, Carl Stokes changed Cleveland for the better. He opened the doors of city hall to Cleveland's marginalized African-American community. Inner city concerns, such as housing, jobs and public services, occupied front and center on the public agenda. Stokes also inspired people to join in reforming society.

Carl Stokes recruited and brought to Cleveland urban planner Norm Krumholz and future Gund Foundation administrator Hank Doll to join his staff. After Stokes left office, they stayed in Cleveland and continued to contribute to various efforts for reform and progressive social change. The example and hope that Stokes brought to city hall inspired activists in other institutions, such as the Catholic church and the early Catholic Commission. Most important of all, Stokes inspired a generation of young African-Americans to become active in politics, civic affairs, and activism.

Republican Ralph Perk replaced Stokes as mayor in 1972 and remained in office until 1977. His was not a happy administration. Perk was hounded by financial problems throughout his administration. One public asset after another – the transit system, the water and sewer systems, and Edgewater Park on the lakefront – were sold off by the strapped city.

Perk seemed to stumble from one embarrassment to another. His wife refused an invitation to the Nixon White House because it conflicted with her bowling night. The nation laughed, but the ethnic community Perk came from understood perfectly. While at an industrial fair, a welding demonstration caught Perk's hair on fire. Again, the nation laughed. Perk tried to use public funds to take the old civic arena off the hands of sports promoter Nick Mileti. The investment and service-starved neighborhoods hit the roof, and the proposal went nowhere. His use of the new community development block grant program flirted with conflicts of interest and violations of both the letter and spirit of the law. His development plans bordered on the bizarre, such as the proposed jetport in Lake Erie. Perk's ill-fated administration became synonymous with a city that appeared to be falling apart at the seams.[7]

Dennis Kucinich was elected in reaction to the mismanagement and blunders of the Perk administration. His election swept aside a number of council members and went down in Cleveland political lore as the "Tuesday Night Massacre." Kucinich centered his administration on his opposition to economic development based on tax abatements and his vow to preserve Cleveland's beleaguered public power company, the Municipal Light and Power Company (Muny Light). Muny Light was a thorn in the side of the privately owned Cleveland Electric Illuminating Co., which was determined to be rid of its historic competitor.

Kucinich inspired progressive urban activists and reformers around the country, who flocked to Cleveland to work in his administration, just as an earlier generation had done for Carl Stokes. Kucinich championed an urban populism that was inspired not only by the civil rights and anti-war movements of the 1960s, but by the legacy of Cleveland's legendary Progressive Era mayor, Tom L. Johnson (1901-1909), who had done battle with the tycoons of his day, just as Kucinich would.

Whereas Stokes enjoyed a brief honeymoon with the corporate and civic establishment, war between Kucinich and the elite began the moment he was sworn in. What followed were two of the most contentious years in the history of Cleveland politics.

Kucinich repeatedly got into trouble because of the behavior of his appointees and aides, who were labeled as young, inexperienced, arrogant, abrasive, and intolerant. Relations with the police department were the same scourge for Kucinich as they had been for previous mayors. Kucinich had brought from San Francisco Richard Hongisto, whom he appointed chief of police. Hongisto had been the darling of the progressive and liberal communities in San Francisco, but he soon ran into trouble with the mayor, who fired him for insubordination in March 1978. It was reminiscent of Carl Stokes's battles with General Davis. Hongisto's firing led to a recall campaign, which Kucinich narrowly survived in August 1978.[8]

The next trial for Kucinich came when the city tried to renegotiate its debt with local banks. M. Brock Weir, CEO of Cleveland Trust, led the corporate coalition against Kucinich. The banks made sale of Muny Light to Cleveland Electric Illuminating Company a condition for rolling over the loans. Kucinich flatly refused, and on the night of December 15, 1978, the City of Cleveland went into default.

Throughout his administration, Kucinich faced the same hostility from city council as Stokes had. While Stokes faced the wrath of white council members led by Council President Jim Staunton, Kucinich confronted Council President George Forbes and a newly empowered African-American block in council, a direct legacy of Stokes. He also was on the receiving end of a blowback from sectors that should have been his allies, such as Cleveland's community organizations, who had become alienated by Kucinich's confrontational politics.

A crisis-weary electorate finally voted Kucinich out of office in 1979 for a candidate who promised to be as conciliatory as Kucinich had been confrontational, republican George Voinovich. Ironically, in the same election that defeated Kucinich, the people of Cleveland soundly defeated a proposal to sell Muny Light. Voinovich was able to make peace with both council and the business elite and take the city out of default. In so doing, his administration was looked upon as boring, but effective and successful.

Kucinich left office a pariah, who nevertheless managed one of the most stunning political comebacks in local history when he returned to Cleveland City Council, then to the state legislature, and finally to the U.S. House of Representatives. What his administration did accomplish was to save Cleveland's public utility. It was an accomplishment that even his past foes were forced to credit to him. Kucinich also revived Cleveland's progressive political tradition so that it could continue to bedevil Cleveland's "great and good" into the future.

Cleveland politics in the 1970s cannot be explained by simply describing the administrations of the mayors who served in that era. It also must take into account Cleveland City Council President George Forbes. Forbes, like Stokes, was a child of the Great Migration. Forbes took advantage of the opportunities opened for African-American politicians by the administration of Carl Stokes, but the manner in which he wielded power was more from the old bare knuckles school of ethnic politics than from the movement ethos of the Stokes years.

Tough, ruthless, abrasive, arrogant, and smarter than everyone around him in council, George Forbes was formidable. He was skilled in the use of rhetoric, patronage, and political fear and intimidation to retain the loyalty of the African-American residents of Cleveland and their elected representatives. His true strength was his alliance with downtown business interests, who valued his ability to deliver support from both the African-American community and city council for their prized projects. It was an arrangement that worked flawlessly from 1973 until 1989, when Forbes was politically retired by one of his former protégés, Michael R. White, who beat him in the 1989 mayoral election. Mayors came and mayors went during Forbes's council presidency, but everyone knew where true political power resided in Cleveland: with George Forbes.

Among the greatest problems that the city faced in the 1970s was the ever-present issue of the Cleveland public schools. The top issue of the decade was desegregation. In 1973 the National Association for the Advancement of Colored People (NAACP) brought suit against the Cleveland public schools for de facto and de jure racial segregation that prevented quality education from reaching all of the system's children. The case finally resulted in a decision on February 6, 1978, by Federal Judge Frank J. Battisti that the Cleveland school system, through decisions on staffing, construction of schools, busing, and assignment of students, had deliberately segregated students. The board responded that it was not the board's fault that housing was segregated. The court was unmoved, and several oversight boards were appointed to supervise the desegregation of Cleveland's schools.

During its subsequent control of the schools, the court issued almost 4,000 separate orders mandating the operation of the schools. Concurrent with this, were two teacher strikes and a semi-permanent financial crisis for the district. The result was a revolving door of one school administrator after another, and an elected board of education whose political antics destroyed its credibility with the citizens of Cleveland, culminating in the mayoral takeover of the board of education by Michael R. White in the 1990s.

Behind all the economic and political events in Cleveland during this period was a power that was never willing to admit to its power: the foundations of Cleveland, especially the Cleveland Foundation and the George Gund Foundation. They have been portrayed as representing everything from disinterested civic good to the cynical manipulation of the public agenda for the benefit of elite interests. Their power has either been overestimated or underestimated.

There are hundreds of foundations in Cleveland, but the undisputed heavy dancers are the Cleveland and Gund Foundations. Both trace their origins to founders of Cleveland Trust.

The Cleveland Foundation was founded in 1914, and is a collection of various bequests, some that are quite specific in their use, and some not. The Cleveland Foundation has funded studies and reform efforts in criminal justice and education, but has generally been the more traditional and conservative of the two. One reason for this is that its decisions are made by a board of trustees who represent a broad range of the moneyed and business leaders of the community.

The Gund Foundation, on the other hand, since its founding in 1952, has reflected the values and interests of Gund family members. The Gund Foundation is far more nimble than its older peer, and far more willing to invest in new policy ventures. The Gund Foundation was very active in the 1970s, helping establish the community organizing movement in Cleveland via its close relationship with the Commission on Catholic Community Action.[9]

This foundation activity would have meant little without the rise of non-profit organizations. Starting in the 1970s and exploding into the 1980s non-profit organizations made the initiatives and priorities of the foundations realities in the communities of Cleveland. They have become virtually equal to local government and corporations in their impact on the lives of Clevelanders. The importance of the Gund and Cleveland Foundations in financing the non-profits has given rise to the accusation that the non-profits are little more than the stalking horses of the foundations, and do not truly reflect the wishes of their alleged constituencies. This position is both understandable and verges upon conspiracy theory. The foundations may not pull all the strings, but they do lay out the concert hall of public policy and vet the orchestra that plays that hall.

The 1970s set the stage and assembled the players who would shape Cleveland's history for the next generation. It was the period when all the problems that had accumulated since the end of the boom times in the 1930s, finally broke over the city.

It seemed that the very environment was turning against Cleveland, starting with the Cuyahoga River catching on fire on June 22, 1969, to declarations by biologists that Lake Erie was dead, to the fierce blizzard of January 26 and 27th, 1978.

With toxic race relations, declining industries, a decrepit educational system, politics as blood sport, housing stock that was literally falling down, and a national reputation as the "mistake on the lake," Cleveland was flat on its back with nowhere to go but up.

In the midst of all this woe, there appeared a popular tee shirt that both recognized the city's plight, and celebrated its tenacious hold on life and the future. The shirt showed the Cleveland skyline buried in snow with a logo declaring, "Cleveland: You Gotta Be Tough." No scholarly study or databank of statistics could better sum up the reality and spirit of Cleveland as it struggled through one of its roughest periods since the Great Depression.

Chapter 2

SEE, JUDGE, ACT:

The Founding of the
Commission on Catholic Community Action.

> The Church is called to demonstrate, by its own community life,
> that every person should be allowed to develop fully, precisely
> because he or she is a person. The Church is also called to be a
> social prophet and catalyst, protesting every injustice, offering
> reasons to hope and motives to serve.
>
> *Empowerment: Skills for Parish Social Action*, Harry Fagan, 1979 [1]

The Commission on Catholic Community Action, the social action arm of the
Catholic Diocese of Cleveland, was critical to the launch of the community
organizing movement. It, in turn, was the product of past activism, both inside and
outside of the church.

Examples of this activism could be seen in the organizing on the east side that
paved the way for the mayoral victory of Carl B. Stokes in 1967. The welfare rights
movement began in Cleveland with a 1966 march from Cleveland to Columbus for
higher benefits, sponsored by the National Welfare Rights Organization (NWRO).
The west side of Cleveland saw organizing by Active Clevelanders Together (ACT),
the West Side Development Corporation, the West Side Citizens for Better Health
Services, Low Income People Together, Citizens to Save Our Metro Health System,
and the Tremont West Development Corporation. Groups such as WELCOME
helped defuse the potential for violence stemming from the desegregation of
Cleveland schools in 1979. All of these movements were beholden to the civil rights
and anti-war movements that shattered the post-war complacency of the 1950s.

Catholic lay organizations such as the Young Christian Students, Young Christian Workers, and the Christian Family Movement influenced the founders of the commission. Rev. Neil Conway was active in the Young Christian Students movement and the Christian Family Movement in Cleveland. He observed:

> They brought a lot of social consciousness to people. They had a simple method: see, judge, and act. They would look at the gospel. They would look at social problems, and would figure out what to do about it.[2]

For Catholic activists, the 1960s began with the Second Vatican Council of the Roman Catholic Church. It revolutionized how the church operated in the modern world. The reforms enacted by the Second Vatican Council opened up opportunities for Catholic social activists that previously would have been unthinkable.

Vatican II Comes to Cleveland

The Second Vatican Council (1963-65), better known as Vatican II, brought the Roman Catholic Church into the modern world. Vatican II legitimized political action in general and political action in the cause of social justice in particular. It changed the way the church operated relative to other religions by allowing the church to enter into ecumenical coalitions and efforts.

Vatican II opened up the hierarchy and was known as "the bishops' council". It gave the bishops of the church a much greater role in integrating church doctrine with practice, and it welcomed lay persons into the day-to-day functioning of the church, especially in writing documents on social problems. [3]

The bishops of the U.S. church took full advantage of these openings. In 1967, the National Conference of Catholic Bishops was formed. Between 1967 and the early 1990s, the conference issued more than 150 statements on social issues in the United States. This was unprecedented in church history. These statements did not speak in bland generalities; they were quite specific in their analysis of problems, and suggested solutions that inspired Catholic activists and legitimized their organizing within the larger community.

As much as Vatican II may have changed the church in Rome, change was far slower at the local level. Bringing Vatican II to Cleveland was a major struggle for liberal Catholics. Their struggle laid the foundation for the Catholic Commission.

An Underground Church

Much of the organizing that led to the formation of the Commission on Catholic Community Action (CCAC) was informal, and included liberal Cleveland area Catholics such as Rev. William Cosgrove, Rev. Neil Conway, and Harry Fagan. They began to meet in the mid-1960s for special Sunday Masses in the basement of St. Henry's Catholic Church, an African-American parish on Cleveland's east side. They called themselves an "underground" church looking for ways to bring Vatican II to Cleveland.

One of the greatest challenges they would face was Cleveland's toxic racial atmosphere. Cleveland was then, and still is, one of the most segregated cities in the country. It had witnessed two major riots. Major battles were waged over segregation in schools and housing. In one incident, a young priest was run over and killed by a bulldozer while protesting the construction of a school that would reinforce school segregation.

The diocese of Cleveland responded to the challenge of racial injustice with the usual conservative timidity at which it was so adept. It allowed formation of a local chapter of the Catholic Interracial Council, which Rev. John LaFarge of New York City formed in 1934 to promote racial tolerance, but only on the condition that it call itself the St. Augustan Guild. When the national Interracial Council held a convention at John Carroll University in Cleveland, it did so without the endorsement of the Cleveland Catholic Diocese.

It was not until Edward Hoban, Bishop of the Diocese of Cleveland, died in 1966 and was replaced by Bishop Clarence Issenmann (1966-1974) that the local interracial council was able to shed its St. Augustan Guild trappings and become the Catholic Interracial Council of Cleveland. It was a step forward in a diocese that would have preferred to avoid the topic altogether. The council was barely founded before people concerned with racism began expressing further frustration with the diocese's timidity in dealing with racism in Cleveland and within the diocese.

Catholic activists repeatedly butted heads with the local church hierarchy over civil rights. They saw other dioceses take a leading role in confronting racism in their communities, but in Cleveland, Catholic leaders protested that they were addressing issues of racial justice through quiet diplomacy behind the scenes. The diocese defended itself by reminding its critics how explosive the issues were in the parishes of Cleveland, and protested that if it took a more forthright public stand, it would only make racial polarization worse and impede progress.

Critics responded that the church displayed little hesitation in telling husbands and wives how they could behave in the bedroom, and showed little timidity in defending its institutional interests. They demanded moral leadership that was unafraid of conflict in the cause of social justice and Christian values.

It wasn't until the administration of Bishop James Hickey (1974-80) that Catholic activists concerned about racism found a sympathetic ear in the chancery offices. Until then, they were on their own. They responded by organizing the Committee for a Council movement.

The Committee for a Council was formed in 1966. It was a lay organization of 150 members who proposed the establishment of a "little council" in the Cleveland Catholic Diocese to implement the policies of Vatican II. The committee worked for two-and-a-half months in early 1966 and produced a series of eight reports on everything from Christian marriage to liturgy.

The report of the Committee for a Council was one of the most important policy documents in the history of the Catholic Diocese of Cleveland. The report cited as a problem the isolation from other races of the Catholic population, especially Catholic suburbanites. The report proposed the establishment of a diocesan office of urban affairs.

The report described the many failures of the church in dealing with racism, such as incidents of racial violence by parish members directed not only at African-Americans, but, in at least one case, at a priest trying to keep the peace. It criticized the training and orientation of priests, claiming that they were better trained for missionary work in foreign countries than for work in the inner cities of the U.S.

The committee addressed its reports to Bishop Issenmann, and sent along petitions in support of creating a council signed by approximately 10,000 parishioners. The response from the diocesan hierarchy was not warm. Rev. Bob Begin, a prominent figure in liberal Catholicism in Cleveland, recalled the bishop's response to the petition:

> The bishop just wouldn't hear anything about it. In fact, he called a compulsory meeting of all the priests of the diocese and had in his hands the petition and threw it across the stage and said, 'Anybody who wants to talk to me, especially the priests, can come to my door and knock. They don't have to sign a petition.'[4]

The church was also profoundly divided over the war in Vietnam. One of the most vocal anti-war activists was Rev. Bob Begin. Begin's interest in the issue began with conversations he had with former students who had just returned from Vietnam. Again, as with the issue of racism, the diocese actively discouraged Catholic peace activists. In 1967, when Begin tried to form a branch of the Catholic Peace Movement, Bishop Issenmann told him to take the word "Catholic" out of it, saying, "This is not a Catholic peace movement. This is your peace movement."

Peace activists, including Begin, made common cause with the broader reform movement in the Cleveland church, as is evident in a statement issued by the Cleveland Catholic Peace Movement on April 10, 1968. In it, the group stated that in spite of official pronouncements on social justice and race relations, the Catholic laity was largely uninvolved in the issues of the day. The task of changing this situation fell to Catholic activists, who found themselves isolated in their parishes.[5]

The year 1968 was spent by Catholic peace activists, promoting educational programs aimed at the Catholic community of Cleveland, even soliciting the involvement of the clergy in a Vietnam Sunday program in October. With the escalation of both the war and the movement against it, there was a feeling among activists that more dramatic actions were called for, and they split from the Cleveland Catholic Peace Movement, to form a new group, Christians Who Care.

In other cities, Catholics were interrupting Masses, demanding that the church address the issue of Vietnam. Begin and Rev. Bernard Meyer disagreed with this tactic. They settled on another tactic: They decided to hold a peace mass at St. John Cathedral, the home church of the diocese on January 26, 1969. Begin described the thinking behind the action,

> Our assumption was that once a Mass had started, no one would dare interrupt it because that's a sin. Our assumption was wrong, so not only did they interrupt it, but they brought the police in and arrested us.[6]

The arrest of Begin and Meyer at St. John Cathedral was one of the most famous anti-war events in Cleveland during the 1960s. The actions of the Cleveland police and the Catholic Diocese created as much controversy as the act itself. There were charges that reporters were roughed up by the police and that one priest stepped on the consecrated host after it had been knocked from Begin's hands. The arrests of Begin and Meyer were looked upon by many as a gross overreaction on the part of the diocese. Begin and Meyer were suspended from the priesthood, further fueling the charges of diocesan overreaction. The hierarchy of the church made Begin and Meyer instant heroes of the local anti-war movement.

The events of January 26 generated responses to the arrests within the peace movement and in the Catholic Interracial Council of Cleveland. A leader of the Cleveland Catholic Peace Movement criticized the overreaction of the diocese, but also denounced Meyer's and Begin's recklessness that threatened to undermine moves being made by the diocese to meet demands of church reformers.

One of the most noteworthy statements issued in response to the incident came from the Catholic Interracial Council of Cleveland whose board unanimously passed a resolution on January 28 that was sympathetic to the mission of Christians Who Care. The board of the council criticized the tactics of Christians Who Care, but expressed an understanding of the frustration that drove the tactics. The board stated:

> We agree with many parts of the statement issued by Christians Who Care. We agree that the diocese of Cleveland has not effectively addressed itself to the role of racism in the white community and in the church. We agree that the church, its officials and members have not treated the problems of the poor with the urgency that they deserve.[7]

The council gave credit to those reformers within the church, but noted that they were still a minority who had received minimal support within the church hierarchy. This caused one of the board members who had not been present at the board vote, to resign in protest, but the resignation did not deter the interracial council from holding firm to its stand. It expressed hope that the diocese would get serious about the concerns of the council.

Frustration was the daily fare of liberal Catholics in the 1960s. Social change is never realistic or practical until it happens. The problem is that those promoting it often fail to recognize the evidence of their successes. Those who were fighting for reform, who represented the anti-war movement and the Catholic Interracial Council and the Committee for a Council, were starting to move the mountain of the local diocesan hierarchy. Probably their greatest accomplishment was the creation of the Catholic Commission. In contrast to past diocesan equivocation and timidity, it was founded on a call for a total response to the challenge of social injustice in Cleveland.

A Total Response: Founding the Commission

Auxiliary Bishop William Cosgrove found himself in the middle of the controversy over the arrests of Begin and Meyer. Begin and Meyer had told him ahead of time about plans for the St. John anti-war Mass. Bishop Cosgrove told them he wished they wouldn't do it because his efforts at reform were starting to bear fruit. He had commissioned a diocesan study by Rev. Dan Reidy, an Akron based priest who was an expert in urban affairs and who would be an early leader of the Commission on Catholic Community Action. Reidy's proposal for a Catholic commission was due to be released in just weeks.

Cosgrove was probably deeply embarrassed by the protest Mass at St. John, because he had announced on January 17 that he would appear at a February 2 forum sponsored by the Cleveland Catholic Peace Movement on the fourteen Milwaukee protesters who had been jailed for burning draft records. This could not have strengthened his position within the diocese. First, he had to deal with the turmoil swirling around the January 26 anti-war Mass, then the release of the founding document of the commission proposing the organization that would be his greatest legacy.

The founding document of the commission was prepared by Rev. Dan Reidy. Cosgrove had noticed Rev. Reidy during the recent riots in the Opportunity Park neighborhood of Akron. Building on his past history of anti-poverty activism in the neighborhood, Reidy had played an honest broker role between the community and the city administration when rioting broke out in response to the assassination of Dr. Martin Luther King, Jr. in April 1968.

Cosgrove met with Reidy, who at the time was working at the Department of Urban Affairs at the University of Akron and was completing a doctoral degree at the University of Pittsburgh. He asked Reidy to do a study of the parishes in the Cleveland diocese, focusing on how they fit into the surrounding neighborhoods and how the diocese could address the issues and problems plaguing the city. The recommendations of the document that Reidy produced led to the founding of the Commission on Catholic Community Action.

In the February 12, 1969, proposal, the argument for the establishment of the commission was made:

> The contemporary crises in American social life need no elaborate analysis here. We have all been witnesses in recent months and years to the great social evils in our national life and our international relations. Our own community has been ravaged by violence, hatred, and great social inequities. Our seeming inability to resolve these great social problems has led to widespread public confusion and much social disruption. We are told, 'America has lost its way'; 'The churches are irrelevant'.[8]

Reidy itemized examples of social failure in continuing poverty, deteriorating neighborhoods and racial strife. He then issued a call to action.

> The time for words has ended. The time for education as our sole major effort has ended, the time for patchwork approaches to inadequate jobs and inadequate housing has ended. We will no longer be part of a half-hearted effort to show our love to our brothers in need. Rather, the problems of human and social blight must be approached with an immediacy, an urgency that means TOTAL RESPONSE.[9]

The document declared the establishment of the Commission on Catholic Community Action (CCCA). The commission would cooperate with all efforts for social justice, evaluate the performance of diocesan institutions "to see that they are measuring up to their fullest capacity to meet the problems of social indignity," and most important, "the Commission will also function as a catalyst to the larger community."

In founding the commission, Reidy wanted a clean break for the new organization with a large role for the laity in the governing board. Cosgrove, was pushing from the other direction to gain the cooperation of traditional institutions, such as Catholic Charities and the Catholic school system, to make the commission work. As Rev. Begin had learned after his protest Mass at St. John Cathedral, one did not get very far making frontal assaults against the church. The work had to be done from the inside of the organization if it were to get anywhere, a lesson Cosgrove knew well. This grated against Reidy's irreverence towards Church bureaucracy.

The document outlined the commission's organizational structure. The formal organization gave it the benefits of being both within the diocese and possessing enough independence to maintain the flexibility of its movement origins. Decisions on the programs and direction of the commission were to be made in internal standing committees and in independent and permanent task forces. Within the task forces, the legacy of the old organizations, such as the Committee for a Council and Christians Who Care, was apparent. Proposed task forces covered the entire panoply of issues, from crime and law enforcement to neighborhoods and social services.

The task forces were unique because they were independent of the commission, yet existed alongside it. The commission wanted the task forces to be free-wheeling centers for give-and-take and experimentation. They were not constrained by being a formal part of the commission or under the control of the church. Both the hierarchy and the task forces found comfort in this arrangement.

One of the greatest assets of the early commission was the unique synergy that existed within its founding staff. The figures who were most powerful in setting the direction of the commission were Auxiliary Bishop William Cosgrove, Rev. Dan Reidy and Harry Fagan. Cosgrove's longtime friends Rev. Neil Conway and Charles Murray joined them. Early in the commission's history, Conway and Murray became active in criminal justice issues, rather than the community organizing activities that dominated the work of Fagan and Reidy. All the same, they were influential in the commission and had come up through the grassroots with Fagan and Cosgrove in building a liberal Catholic constituency within the church hierarchy.

Cosgrove was the father figure, protector, and spiritual mentor of the commission. Reidy was its intellectual, theoretician, and strategist. Fagan was the commission's salesperson and public relations person.

Auxiliary Bishop William Cosgrove thrived in the atmosphere created by Vatican II. He was committed to social justice before Vatican II legitimized it. His first experience with activism was union organizing, when he helped organize custodial workers in the county hospital system. Cosgrove and Neil Conway were also active in the organizing drive to unionize the custodial staff of St. Luke's Hospital in the 1960s.[10]

Conway described Cosgrove as a Dorothy Day/Catholic Worker type of ascetic. Cosgrove played a unique role in the church, which made him indispensable in the founding of the commission. According to Reidy:

> Cosgrove was the protector of it. He was the head person.
> Everyone realized that the commission was his baby. He made sure
> that it had a high and positive profile in the Catholic bureaucracy.
> He got funding for it. He allowed it to grow, and during the time
> we were connected, it kept growing with size and influence.[11]

Cosgrove was wise enough to give his managers the freedom to run the commission. Bishop Cosgrove was a loyal member of the institutional church, and he knew how to operate in that setting. He did not favor criticism of the church hierarchy, and he would tell critics that they (the church hierarchy) have their job, and we have ours.[12] His role as an organization man of the traditional church and his attention to traditional religious duties enabled Cosgrove to sell the idea of the commission to a church hierarchy that had heretofore resisted similar such efforts as too radical. Rev. Reidy said of Cosgrove:

> By the force of energy, he was able to get these things done. He was well liked beforehand. He was a very social guy. He was an athlete. He was a golfer, he played baseball, handball. He was well liked by the clergy. Even clergy who weren't interested in social justice liked him as a person. So when he'd be leaning on them to do something, they remembered the guy they played golf with who was one of the boys.[13]

According to Reidy, Cosgrove's passion was social justice. He recalled:

> He was a very courageous person and was strongly committed to doing something positive in social justice. He saw the CCCA as a vehicle to do that. These programs weren't service programs. He saw them as prophetic acts, like the Old Testament prophets. What we were to do was to do some courageous prophetic acts.[14]

Cosgrove was not particularly interested in community organizing, Reidy said:

> He wasn't interested in community organizing for its own sake or changing government. But he allowed those of us who thought it was a good way to promote social justice to do it, and protected us from criticism and attack.[15]

Also important in Cosgrove's ability to act was the support he received from Bishop James Hickey (1974 to 1980). In 1974, Hickey succeeded Bishop Issenmann, whose main contribution to the founding of the commission was to leave it alone and to give Cosgrove a free hand.

Hickey offered active support. The commission was unique within the American Catholic church. For Hickey, it was a source of pride, and he regularly promoted it in meetings of the U.S. Council of Catholic Bishops. At these gatherings, he would bring along Cosgrove and Fagan and have them describe the work of the commission. According to Neil Conway, having Hickey in charge of the diocese was a stroke of supreme good luck for the commission in its infancy.

Rev. Dan Reidy became one of the intellectual architects of not only the commission, but of the entire strategy that would launch the community organizing movement with Project Interface and the Buckeye Woodland Community Congress. Reidy's contributions are largely unknown to all but the earliest veterans of the era. He left Cleveland and the church in 1976, and his reputation was rapidly eclipsed by Fagan's.

Reidy grew up in the western suburbs of Cleveland and took an early interest in the civil rights movement. He volunteered at Karamu House, the African-American cultural center on the east side of Cleveland, while going to school. From 1965 to 1969, he lived in Akron, doing graduate work at the Center for Urban Studies at the University of Akron. While in Akron, he lived in the African-American neighborhood of Opportunity Park and was active in War on Poverty programs in the neighborhood.

The first person to serve as executive director of the commission soon left the position. Reidy was his replacement. While no one doubted Reidy's ability to offer the commission a vision or initial strategy, he did not receive rave reviews as a manager.

Reidy could be abrasive. He was almost anti-clerical in his attitudes, and he had little regard for the church hierarchy. Fagan thought Reidy was an ineffective Lone Ranger. Conway said Reidy would provide finances and analysis, but for support, you went to Cosgrove.

The relationship between Cosgrove and Reidy was that of a mentor and a brilliant student. The relationship between Reidy and Fagan was much more complex, with hints of sibling rivalry. Those who witnessed the relationship either said that it was warm and close, or that there was conflict between the two. There was mention of Reidy starting to feel jealous of Fagan's meteoric rise within the commission.

While Reidy gave the early commission intellectual integrity and vision, he was not the one to carry that to the larger community. A salesperson was needed, and that salesperson was Fagan. Fagan was a native Clevelander whose family ran bars and restaurants. At the time he became active in church organizing, he was working in the advertising department of the Plain Dealer and living in University Heights with his family. In trying to describe how Harry became Harry, his friend Neil Conway explained that you had to understand that Harry was raised behind a bar.[16] Gregarious, fun loving, a renowned conversationalist, Fagan was intensely interested in people. The social skills he possessed were made to order for the work he would perform for the commission.

He was very successful at advertising, but it did not fit in with his real interests. Working for the commission did because it involved him with his passion, which was people. He did not consider working for the commission to be work. It was fun. Along with the idealism and the enjoyment of working with people, Fagan was driven by other desires. He wanted to be somebody. He wanted his life to have a greater purpose than just selling ads. And, most prophetically, he was convinced that he would not live long. He told people that longevity did not run in his family. Both his father and grandfather had died young. He would ask people who were close to him, "What would you want to do if someone told you that you only had six months to live?"[17]

Genes aside, his lifestyle did not favor a long life. Fagan, according to Conway, was a bohemian. He loved to party, he drank too much, he chain smoked cigarettes, he had a horrible diet, he hung out at jazz clubs, and he was a workaholic. When he assumed supervisory duties at the commission after Reidy's departure, he said that what he was looking for in a staff person was a "workaholic with values who liked to have a couple of beers after work as well."[18] An informal group of Catholic activists that Fagan was a part of was called Beer and Bibles. Participants combined scriptural readings and discussions with what could only be called a happy hour. When the commission was underway with its first burst of organizing, Fagan hosted socials at the bar his parents founded in the Flats, Fagan's, where staff from the commission and organizers could meet informally, discuss their work, and kick around ideas for future campaigns.

Above all, his talents were as a salesperson. Holly Gigante, a Catholic nun who worked for the early commission, described Fagan's skills:

> He knew what result he wanted, which an organizer often does. You have a trick in each pocket and you know what you want to get. What you want is the group to take ownership and make some decisions. You wanted the impetus. You want people to leave with homework and know what they're doing.[19]

Action for a Change: The Commission's First Great Success

With a structure and a staff in place, the Catholic Commission needed an initial project that would put it on the map of Cleveland institutions. That project was Action for a Change. It was an experiential education project focused on Cleveland parishes whose members would attend a series of educational forums and discussion groups designed to explore the many social issues that were foremost on the public agenda at the time. The program was in six parts, each taking on a new subject, such as housing, jobs, welfare.

Program organizers tried to follow the methodology of Paulo Freire, the renowned Brazilian educator, social activist, and critic. Freire based his educational philosophy on dialogue between educators and those being educated. The educator did not lecture: He or she worked with students. Lessons came from examining the lived experience of those involved. The goal of the process was action to make change, enhance community, and build social capital.[20]

A priority of the program was racism. The program focused on giving white, suburban, middle class people a taste of the realities that inner city poor people were experiencing. The seminars were held throughout the city and were televised on the local public television affiliate, WVIZ. Between 5,000 and 10,000 people went through the experience. Fagan explained:

We were trying to say, we don't care where you come in on that conversation. The point is there's something wrong. No matter what issue you look at, people get screwed. You've got to go one step deeper. [21]

A key part of the experience was field trips and exercises, such as filling out a form to apply for welfare benefits. These exercises put people into contact with the daily problems faced by residents of the inner city.

It also made the commission a place where people came for help in combating social problems and injustices ranging from housing discrimination to the redlining of inner-city neighborhoods. It provided institutional cover and resources to Cleveland activists wanting to organize a grassroots response to the many problems of a troubled city.

As Cleveland moved into the 1970s, it possessed in the Commission on Catholic Community Action what it had not seen since the Congress of Industrial Organizations (CIO) in the 1930s or the African-American churches of the 1950s and 60s: an institutional launching pad for social change activism.

The stage was now set for launching a movement.

Chapter 3

Establishing a Model: The Buckeye Woodland Community Congress.

We were making history. We were going to make a revolution in Cleveland. People on a staff level believed the mythology that they were part of writing history. There was a group of committed people who said 'All this is fun.' The spirit of the moment captured the imagination of other neighborhoods in Cleveland.

Joe Mariano, *Buckeye Woodland Community Congress*[1]

All movements for social change are linked in the public mind to one or two prominent organizations. The Southern Christian Leadership Conference (SCLC) and the Student Non-Violent Coordinating Committee (SNCC) represented the civil rights movement in the South. Students for a Democratic Society (SDS) was synonymous with the student and anti-Vietnam War movements of the 1960s. When people thought of the movement to organize farm workers in California, they thought of the United Farm Workers.

In a similar way, one organization represented to the public the community organizing that swept through Cleveland's neighborhoods. That organization was the Buckeye Woodland Community Congress (BWCC).

There were many organizations that survived longer than Buckeye Woodland

Community Congress, won as many victories, and produced as many activists and leaders. However, no other organization cast as large a shadow, blazed as many trails with important issues, or served as an example that inspired people to organize as BWCC did. The movement it represented rose and flourished as Buckeye rose and flourished, and declined and died, as Buckeye declined and died.

Project Interface 1973-1974

Buckeye Woodland Community Congress was an experiment that became a model. The neighborhood in which it developed was a difficult testing ground. It was famous for its Hungarian community, but included Slovaks, and Italians, as well. These competing ethnic groups were united in their animosity to the newest group to settle in the neighborhood: African-Americans. Msgr. Geno Baroni, a hero of the Catholic Commission, remembered with despair a visit he made to the Buckeye neighborhood because of the level of explicit racism and hatred he found.[2] If community organizing could work in the Buckeye-Woodland neighborhood, it could work anywhere. It all started with Project Interface.

Project Interface provided the commission with an opportunity to succeed in organizing in Cleveland's neighborhoods after efforts to organize African-Americans in the Glenville neighborhood and Hispanics living on the Near West Side ended in utter failure.[3] The commission was accused of paternalism and a heavy handed top down approach in these failed efforts. Underlying all these efforts was the toxic racial and ethnic atmosphere of Cleveland, which was played as a zero sum game where the advance of one group, could only be purchased by harm to another.

Rev. Dan Reidy was interested in finding a neighborhood in which he could organize to unite diverse racial and ethnic groups around common problems. It was an interest shared by the rest of the commission. He termed it "urban ethnic organizing", which had been promoted on a national level by Msgr. Baroni. Reidy thought the Buckeye-Woodland neighborhood would be ideal for his experiment. He recalled:

> I became intrigued by the Buckeye Woodland area. I suggested that it would be a good place to try some crossover community organizing. You had black people. It was an Italian neighborhood. It was the mother neighborhood of the Hungarians. There was an overlap of the Slovaks. It was on the edge of Ludlow, young, single professional white types who weren't ethnically based. It seemed to me it had opportunities. [4]

One of the flash points for social conflict in Buckeye-Woodland was crime. Buckeye residents were alarmed by the rise of street crime involving young African-Americans. This heightened the already tense racial atmosphere of the neighborhood. Private militia units, such as the Buckeye Special Police, were formed. The

Catholic church was drawn into this issue because of the presence in this organization of several local priests. The city, the police, and the church were alarmed at the chaos that could result from vigilante activity. The diocese told Bishop Cosgrove to deal with this explosive situation. He investigated, and the priests who had joined the Buckeye Special Police were persuaded to resign.

Bishop Cosgrove recognized that the crisis in Buckeye-Woodland not only represented a danger, but also an opportunity. Here was a chance for the commission to redeem itself with an organizing project that could defuse the tinderbox. His entrée was that the ethnic communities of Buckeye-Woodland were overwhelmingly Catholic.[5]

The first step taken was when local parishes founded the Buckeye Woodland Catholic Community Council. The council focused on three issues. The first was conditions at Audubon Junior High School, including the maintenance of the school, unruly students at the school menacing neighbors, and inadequate educational conditions at the school, which, since the early 1960s, had been predominantly African-American. The community council established a task force on the problems of the school, and the result was the first community meeting attended by white ethnics and African-Americans. The second issue was the founding of a Catholic kindergarten to which white ethnic parents would feel comfortable sending their children. The third was housing. Housing problems in the neighborhood ran from block busting to abuses of the Federal Home Administration program. As with the Audubon issue, the housing issue drew support from both ethnic and African-American communities.[6]

A pastoral planning process surveyed the problems of the area and the state of its existing community organizations and institutions. No existing group was capable or interested in bringing the community together to deal with common problems. The Buckeye Woodland Catholic Community Council was limited by being a Catholic organization. If the goal was to create an inclusive organizing process, a broader effort was needed. The only alternative was to start a new organization to take on the task of organizing the Buckeye neighborhood. The next step for Rev. Reidy was Project Interface.

Reidy worked with Ken Kovach, an Orthodox seminarian, who had grown up in the neighborhood. Kovach and Reidy laid out a proposal to the Campaign for Human Development to fund Project Interface.

The Campaign for Human Development (CHD) was founded in 1969 as the brainchild of a leading light of liberal Catholicism during this time, Monsignor Geno Baroni. Baroni, pastor of an African-American church in Washington, DC, had courted the displeasure of the church hierarchy by marching with Martin Luther King in Selma, Alabama, and had become an expert on the issues of the inner city and race relations. He finished his public life as an undersecretary at the Department of Housing and Urban Development under President Jimmy Carter.

In the tumultuous days after the assassination of Martin Luther King and the resulting rioting, Baroni feared that ethnic urban Catholics could provide a mass base for a racist reactionary movement in the United States. What was needed was a campaign to work in communities that were now pitted against one another and to unite them on the basis of common problems, interests, and issues. His goal in convincing the National Conference of Catholic Bishops to start the campaign was to fund the organization of poor ethnic and minority communities to work together for economic and social power through an annual fund drive.

The Campaign for Human Development became a prime source for seed money for many organizing efforts in Cleveland and around the country. It has a special place within the philanthropic world. As Shel Trapp of National People's Action (NPA) put it, "The CHD helps to fund dreams."

Kovach wanted to build Project Interface using as a foundation the intense sense of community which nurtured him while growing up in the Buckeye-Woodland area. While this intense form of community was an asset, it was also a problem for those who wished to keep the peace when newcomers entered the neighborhood. A community may be comforting for insiders while erecting a wall of hostility to outsiders or those who do not fit in.

Project Interface began in the summer of 1973 with the formation of the sponsoring organization, the Buckeye Woodland Community Council. This council was made up of members of the Buckeye Woodland Catholic Community Council and the East End Community Development Foundation, which withdrew early from the project because of internal problems. Funding Project Interface with a Campaign for Human Development grant was no problem. Reidy was CHD's diocesan director in Cleveland.

Tom Gannon, who had worked as a full-time organizer in California and Indiana for the United Farm Workers, was hired as the project's lead organizer, along with Greg Groves, an African-American organizer. Gannon, through his work with the United Farm Workers was a direct link with people such as Caesar Chavez, Fred Ross, Delores Huerta, and Marshall Gans, who had been trained by the intellectual guru of the community organizing movement, Saul Alinsky.

Alinsky started out in the 1930s in Chicago as an organizer for the Packinghouse Workers of the Congress of Industrial Organizations (CIO). He took the lessons learned from that experience to organize the neighborhood so many packing house workers lived in, the Back of the Yards. In the following years, he helped organize migrant farm workers in California, where his influence was seminal for the young Caesar Chavez, founder of the United Farm Workers (UFW).

Alinsky was also instrumental in organizing against racism in Rochester, New York. He founded the Industrial Areas Foundation that carried on his philosophy of organizing after his death in 1972. That philosophy was based on mobilizing the powerless around issues of self interest. It took the old bare-knuckles style of union organizing he learned in the CIO and applied it to communities. His books, *Rules for Radicals* and *Reveille for Radicals*, were required reading in community organizing circles in Cleveland and throughout the country.

In the first quarterly report to the Campaign for Human Development, Project Interface laid out its organizing strategy, which emphasized mass-based, multi-issue organizing for basic social change. It would strive to preserve the distinctiveness of existing communities and organizations, and to be sensitive to ethnic and cultural issues. Underlying all activity would be a commitment to the values of human dignity, liberation, and social justice.[7]

The goal of Project Interface was to form a community congress to incorporate and unite the myriad organizations, street clubs, nationality groups, and churches in the Buckeye-Woodland neighborhood.

The first step of Project Interface was to send its organizers to undergo training with the National Center for Urban Ethnic Affairs (NCUEA), the National Housing Training Center (later the National Training and Information Center of National People's Action), and the Movement for Economic Justice.

The second step was a series of interviews and meetings with established agencies and organizations by Gannon and Groves to introduce Project Interface and to find out what these groups were up to. They were not warmly greeted. First, there was the traditional paranoia that sets in with established groups when they feel they must defend their turf against an interloper. Then there was the traditional hostility that existed between traditional social work and community organizing.

The organizers did not just interview existing groups; they also targeted the unorganized part of the Buckeye-Woodland community, and sought to start new organizations. The initial issues developed by Gannon and Groves in this first period were tenant issues at the Woodhill Homes and neighboring Cleveland Metropolitan Housing Authority (CMHA) estates and dilapidated structures that were being ignored by the city. Groves canvassed 400 units in the Woodhill Homes housing project of CMHA and organized a tenants' organization that took on CMHA over issues of mismanagement, maintenance, and other failings.

Project Interface dealt with issues that were classics in the field and usually centered on the failure of city hall to provide public services, such as animal control, slow police response time, failure to inspect dilapidated houses and buildings, and traffic control. When city hall fell down on these duties, the community organizations had issues around which to mobilize.

Project Interface also encountered new, more difficult issues. In 1974, the issue of panic peddling of homes became a concern, with realtors using racial fears to stimulate home sales. It was one of the early instances when Project Interface had to deal with a racially divisive issue. Gannon described the problem in his February 12-28, 1974, report to Rev. Reidy:

> I've been checking out the reports of questionable real estate practices in the area. I have two examples of real estate letters distributed in the community.
>
> I am attempting to organize some blacks in the upper end to

approach these realtors and I want to avoid any racial confrontation. I don't want to have whites screaming at blacks.[8]

Gannon began to research the issue and the behavior of real estate agents in the area. The neighborhood at the time was being canvassed by real estate brokers who would leave leaflets and business cards at houses, soliciting business. Real estate agents even called Barb Pertz, a future leader of Buckeye Woodland Community Congress, who was renting an apartment at the time.

> They wanted to know if I wanted to sell my home. They would use words like, 'The neighborhood is changing.' This is how cocky they were at the time: 'You want to get money, the value of your house now before something happens,' 'If you wait, you might not get what your house is worth.' 'We've got a buyer for your home.' It was unbelievable.[9]

Pertz credited the African-American residents of Buckeye-Woodland for joining the effort.

> It wasn't just white people going to the agents; it was black people, too. I have a feeling black people were saying, 'We don't want this. We want a mixed neighborhood, an interracial neighborhood. We don't want this white flight.' I have to give a lot of credit to the blacks in Buckeye-Woodland because they stood up and said, 'We want you to stop this, too.'[10]

With publicity and visits by community delegations to the realtors responsible, the level of panic peddling fell off to the point where it was no longer a burning issue. Probably the greatest accomplishment of the campaign was how it demon-strated African-American and white cooperation on an issue that could have very easily gone the other way.

Public transportation issues were also central to the neighborhood. The Buckeye-Woodland neighborhood had a high concentration of the elderly poor. This led to one of the most significant campaigns for organizers of this period: transportation services for the elderly. The strategic opportunity was the creation of the new Regional Transit Authority in 1975. How this new transit system was organized would establish public transportation policy for decades. Key demands were fares for the elderly and disabled and the preservation of the dial-a-bus system that picked up passengers at their homes when called. The dial-a-bus system had been a victory for senior citizen activists in 1974.

The campaign founded the city-wide Senior Citizens Transportation Coalition, which, in turn, became the Senior Citizens Coalition (SCC). This campaign demonstrated a behind-the-scenes alliance between the City Planning Commission under planning director Norm Krumholz, and groups such as the future Buckeye Woodland Community Congress. As Krumholz described it:

> Over the years, a symbiotic relationship had developed: The senior coalition had learned to trust us, and we had learned to use their organizational power to achieve common objectives. Calls to the Senior Citizens Coalition to inform them of transit meetings, to lay out the issues, to advise them on strategy, and to coordinate their transportation to meetings were undoubtedly worth more in Cleveland than [were] invitations to Planning Commission meetings and discussions of general, unfocused objectives.[11]

The activism of the seniors disturbed the technocrats, politicians, and representatives of such elite institutions as the Growth Association and law firms such as Squire Sanders and Dempsey. They were accustomed to meeting behind closed doors with their peers to set the course of events for the city. They were not prepared, for example, for the seniors to attend a December meeting of the RTA board and hold an impromptu Christmas party. Gannon, lead organizer for the future Buckeye Woodland Community Congress, described the action:

> They were in a meeting in a closed door session, and one of the organizers had rewritten some of the Christmas carols with RTA and dial-a-bus lyrics. We were serenading RTA board members with "Dial-a-bus, dial-a-bus, coming down the street, - RTA is stopping you because they are too cheap." You know, to "Jingle Bells." Then we had Christmas cookies that we wanted to present to the board, baked in the shape of a dial-a-bus. They went nuts, but we finally won.[12]

The City Planning Commission, in alliance with such groups as the Senior Citizens Coalition, won a great deal of what they wanted in the policies of the new transit system. These included the preservation of the old dial-a-bus, to be renamed Community Responsive Transit (CRT).[13]

To Gannon, the CRT buses are an enduring legacy of this campaign:

> I think that was one of the more successful campaigns. Your grandmother or aunt could call and get a ride. Every time I see those buses and I see senior citizens get off, it makes me feel pretty good about organizing because that was a long-term victory that we won. We always dream about those kind of victories.[14]

Groves left Project Interface, and Gannon called on Joe Mariano. Mariano had worked with Gannon during his days with the United Farm Workers Union. Mariano was still working in California, but he was restless and wanted to move on to other organizing work. He described Gannon's enticements to come east from San Francisco:

> He told me that they were doing this project on the southeast side of Cleveland: 'There's blacks, Hungarians, and Italians; we're bringing people together around issues.' I grew up in Newark, and if that's the case, I want to see it. I knew all the tensions that had existed in Newark with the ethnics and blacks. The icing on the cake was, we got this guy coming out who knew Saul Alinsky. I said, 'I'll be there October 23, 1974.' [15]

Two of the people to whom Gannon introduced Mariano were Shel Trapp, lead organizer for National People's Action, and Harry Fagan. Mariano and his wife, Karen Nielson, were introduced to Trapp at the airport before he caught a flight:

> It was a balding guy in a 1950s suit. He (Trapp) said, 'Do you have any organizing experience?' Karen Nielson was with me at the time.
>
> I said that I was with the UFW. Then Karen said, 'No.' He [Trapp] told Gannon to get the map out. He said to me; 'You got any problems working with white racists? You work over here with the Italians.'
>
> He said to Karen, 'You got any problems working with blacks?' Before she could answer, he said, 'You work over here. I'll be back in two weeks to tell you exactly what you're going to do.'

The next day they were introduced to Harry Fagan. Mariano described the meeting:

> The next day, we talked to Harry Fagan, who was a breeze compared to Trapp. Gannon said, 'Tell him you like building coalitions.' I didn't know what that was about. I said, 'I want to find out about building coalitions.' Harry said, 'You're the man.' [16]

Everything Trapp had promised to Mariano and Nielson was true, and then some. The area that Mariano was organizing was wracked by white flight, racial tensions and suspicions, and a perception of being forgotten by the city.

> I found that the people were bailing out of the neighborhood. I did a lot of door knocking. The folks in Mt. Carmel would literally be

packing up their belongings, saying 'You're five years too late. Where the hell were you?' 'The neighborhood is changing, and I am getting out.' That was a lot of the attitude. Those folks who wanted to stay did for two reasons. One, they had no choice. Two, they were determined to stay and fight, see their neighborhood resurge.[17]

Buckeye Woodland Community Congress was sold as an organization that could maximize the power of the constituent groups without destroying their autonomy. United in the form of a congress, they would be taken much more seriously by foundations, corporations, and government.

The kickoff event for the public drive for a congress was a speech that future congresswoman Barbara Milkulski gave to an audience of 150 in the Buckeye Woodland neighborhood on June 14, 1974. Most of the audience were activists with Project Interface, but representatives from other neighborhoods were present, as well.

Milkulski was a representative with the South East Community Organization of Baltimore, and spoke about the experiences of community congresses in Baltimore, Chicago, Milwaukee, and in Cleveland with the Heights Community Congress. She was from a neighborhood very much like Buckeye-Woodland. She had instant legitimacy with those attending.

The campaign for a community congress was on. By October 1974, a call to found a congress had been issued to the community at large, complete with a set of letters and leaflets explaining the rationale for founding the Buckeye Woodland Community Congress.

Racial divisions and politics not only presented a challenge to organizing the congress; they were also used to get people organized for the founding convention in February 1975. Joe Mariano described what he used to turn people out:

> I was having problems getting the Fairwood neighborhood excited. They could have had a delegation of thirty: I had maybe fifteen people signed up. Trapp said, 'I'll be in for the last meeting; do a little rah-rah talk about the convention. Have the meeting at the East End Community House: the whites will feel safe there. Have it in a small room, a basement, ...'

> There were a shitload of black folks in the room, at least fifty black and twenty-five white. The reason they [whites] turned out more people was they realized they weren't going to get anyone elected to the board. The Hungarians went crazy and started turning people out.

The result of the mobilization of the white ethnic residents was a board that was dominated by them. Example is a great teacher, however, and soon the African-American residents became skilled at internal organization politics. Mariano described their education:

> People like to get elected and control things. Two years down the road, the blacks realized how they could take over. They were clearly more than fifty per cent; somehow, the organization didn't represent them equally. They made their deals. Some of the white ethnics would tell the blacks, 'I want you on my ticket for vice-president.' All these deals were being cut.[18]

The founding convention of the Buckeye Woodland Community Congress was held on February 15, 1975, at Benedictine High School. The convention was a rousing success, with 700 delegates representing 105 organizations in attendance and numerous politicians and other community leaders present to wish them well. The convention passed bylaws, and elected an initial slate of leaders to serve in a congress senate and executive board.

Buckeye Woodland's founding attracted the attention of the city and sparked the imagination of activists everywhere. Ken Kovach described its importance:

> We were actually the first coalition of community groups in the city of Cleveland to be established. I think the Catholic Commission was looking for a model. Buckeye Woodland was a good model because, subsequently, the commission helped support the development of many other community congresses in the St. Clair-Superior area and in the Broadway area.[19]

Not only was Buckeye Woodland Community Congress (BWCC) one of the first community coalitions to form and to get the attention of the city, but was also noted for the quality of its activism. BWCC was known for its ability to focus, its militancy, its skill at getting publicity, and the fact that it was absolutely relentless once it had targeted an issue or a foe. Gannon commented on its uniqueness:

> It was one of the few neighborhoods, at that time, where blacks and whites actually did come together and network together in an organization. It wasn't tied to existing institutions like Neighborhood Centers Association or United Areas Citizens Agencies and some of those groups.

> We could afford to be a lot more...militant. We had a reputation as a group that could pull people together, that was hard-nosed, that meant business, that we would come after you, that would not be

satisfied, but knew what they wanted and had well-focused issues.[20]

Sharon Bryant, another leader, described BWCC's expertise:

> We were good at what we did; and we shared it. It wasn't a big-headed mess of just a few people. Everybody did something. If it was just something geared to the street corner, we celebrated. Everybody celebrated, working together and we shared the victories. That's the most important thing.[21]

Buckeye Woodland Community Congress focused on issues that all the other groups would deal with. It was one of the first community organizations in the country to file a Community Reinvestment Act (CRA) complaint. It was influential in shaping the Regional Transit Authority (RTA) by helping organize the Senior Citizens Coalition.

Buckeye focused attention on the abuse of Community Development Block Grant (CDBG) moneys, when it opposed the sale of the old Arena in 1975. Buckeye, working with National People's Action (NPA), forced revisions in Federal Home Administration (FHA) policies concerning the reimbursement of homeowners who had bought FHA houses thinking they were up to code when they were not.

There were two other areas in which BWCC's influence dominated. First, veterans of the group went on to become trainers and staff people for the Catholic Commission, and helped found and develop new community organizations throughout the city. Gannon was instrumental in launching the St. Clair Superior Coalition (SCSC) and Citizens to Bring Broadway Back (CBBB). Other veterans of BWCC such as George Barany, went on to staff the Senior Citizen Coalition and the Ohio Training Center.

The second area in which BWCC was influential was in providing a ready-made manual for other groups on how to get started. Barany described BWCC's example:

> All these groups basically copied the Campaign for Human Development proposal that Buckeye first put in. Here was the Buckeye model, and if you want to do something in your neighborhood, here's how you do it, and then it gave very direct assistance. Here's a file that says, here's how you get money, here's how you get people, here are flyers, this is how you organize a street club...[22]

There was a downside to Buckeye's reputation. It had a spirit that went beyond esprit de corps, into an arrogant, overbearing attitude of superiority that many other groups found alienating. BWCC portrayed itself as the roughest and the toughest group in town, the group that produced the greatest number of people for hits, (as acts of civil disobedience were called). It positively gloried in the recklessness of its confrontational style.

Inez Killingsworth of Union Miles Community Coalition (UMCC) commented that BWCC knew no fear, and that a frequent comment in the aftermath of an action was that the group had once again done something crazy.[23]

Barany and fellow BWCC veteran Pat Kinney, commented on Buckeye's spirit run amok. Barany recalled one event, in particular:

> I can remember, one planning meeting where we walked in with sixty leaders. Harry Fagan, chaired the meeting, and got very nervous because of our demand that the first neighborhood conference be held at Buckeye. He basically got the body to vote that each organization would have one vote. He was determined that the first neighborhood conference would not be at Buckeye. It was actually held down at the office of the Catholic Diocese.[24]

To Kinney, Buckeye was cocky:

> We produced a lot of people, did a lot of things, but we kind of lived and breathed that. If you were an organization of twenty people and you only brought twenty people to everything and it doesn't matter if it was the biggest issue in the world, a medium issue, then the response was, 'What's going on? Why can't you get more people in your neighborhood to come to things?' If you were always there and you brought 200 people and you were thinking, 'Well, we're the big producers.' That's what I mean by 'cocky'. [25]

Arrogance and cockiness have their places at times. Buckeye could not have launched the community organizing movement in Cleveland had it been humble and polite. Such efforts require a certain level of brazenness and even, as Killingsworth commented, craziness to break through the suffocating inertia of the status quo. However it may have grated on some, there was no doubt that Buckeye did launch the movement.

Chapter 4

BUILDING THE GROUPS

Within five years of Buckeye Woodland Community Congress's (BWCC) founding, community organizations had formed throughout Cleveland. One important factor behind this phenomenal growth was the friendship and alliance between Harry Fagan, and Henry "Hank" Doll, program officer of the George Gund Foundation.

Doll was a Presbyterian minister who worked in a wide range of positions in Cleveland at the Cleveland Foundation, in the administration of Mayor Carl Stokes, and for the Greater Cleveland Interchurch Council. His specialty was working both sides of the street: for foundations and for the non-profit organizations. He was interested in pursuing the community organizing ideas of Saul Alinsky that he had been introduced to at the University of Pittsburgh.

He found the opportunity to put those ideas into action when he was hired by the Gund Foundation and began his association with Fagan. As Doll recalled, they had a meeting of the minds about the about the possible uses of organizing:

> I think both Harry and I agreed that there was a need for commu-
> nity organizing prior to doing development work. You had to have
> the neighborhood people coalesce around issues and ideas; there-
> fore, you had to have community organizing activities going on.[1]

The primary vehicle of the Catholic Commission's work in the neighborhoods was the Training and Technical Assistance (T&TA) program funded by the Gund Foundation. The program began in 1978 and provided consultants, trainers, and outside experts to help the neighborhood movement grow and develop.

The agenda for the first year of the T & TA program was building the groups through individual consultations among trainers, leaders, and organizers in city-wide training sessions. Much of the work was dedicated to building block clubs, recruiting members, running meetings, and developing issues.

One of the most important trainers in Cleveland was Karen Nielson, who began to work at the commission when she and Joe Mariano left BWCC in 1978. Working with consultants such as Shel Trapp, Nielson trained a generation of organizers who had had little to no exposure to the organizing experiences of the 1960s. Bob Pollack of Near West Neighbors called his generation "the little brothers and sisters of the New Left" who had missed out on all the action. It was the trainer's job to launch these novices into a very tough field. Linda Hudecek described her baptism by fire, presided over by Nielson:

> I can remember a blizzard, and she dropped me off on the street and said, 'I'll pick you up in an hour and you'd better have ten names.' I was door knocking during the middle of a blizzard and she was just really very focused about the steps and stages you go through to do block clubs. Karen was very committed to block club organizing. She was very, very good at teaching me how to go through those steps and holding my hand through each phase.[2]

Nielson's memory of dumping Linda on the street was a little different:

> They came in and said 'We're not dressed.' I said, 'Good God, you're all supposed to have long underwear, rubber boots, and mittens and I am not your mother!' There was no excuse. You were supposed to be out there. We were ruthless.[3]

One concern expressed by the trainers was the culture of organizing in Cleveland and whether the staff and leadership of the groups really knew what the movement was all about. In order to meet this challenge, the T&TA program sponsored a weekend retreat at Punderson State Park. The workshop was led by an experienced organizer, Tom Gaudette, who had been trained by Alinsky. It was not only a training session; it was a process of group bonding.

The groups were growing with twelve separate groups reported in the 1979 T & TA proposal. They hosted a meeting of the National Commission on Neighborhoods and the first of several citywide neighborhoods conferences.

The Community Organizations of Cleveland

The best way to get an accurate picture of the process of organizing in Cleveland is to look at the history and development of some of the most important groups of the time.

The St. Clair Superior Coalition

One of the commission's first successes in organizing after BWCC was the St. Clair Superior Coalition (SCSC). The coalition began in January 1976, when four of its future leaders attended a seminar on housing issues and community organizing at Cleveland State University. At the same seminar was Tom Gannon, recently from BWCC. Taking note of what other neighborhoods, particularly Buckeye, were doing, these leaders decided that the way to go to address their neighborhood's problems was to organize a group, as well.

The spring of 1976 was a period of building. The organizers of St. Clair met with representatives of BWCC. They had much in common, with both groups working in racially conflicted neighborhoods on such issues as housing and crime.

A name was chosen, the St.Clair-Superior Coalition (SCSC), boundaries were established, and work began to bring in members and to form block clubs. The infant organization decided on its top three priorities: housing, youth, and crime. Gannon was assigned by the commission to work with the coalition.

Sr. Clair's application to the Campaign for Human Development was approved. A $3,000 grant enabled SCSC to hire its first organizer. The summer saw victories with improved police services, the demolition of several problem properties, and the founding of more block clubs.

One of the basics of community organizing as promoted by National People's Action (NPA) and practiced in Cleveland was a heavy emphasis on block club organizing. Bill Gruber, one of the early organizers of SCSC, described the dynamics of "door knocking" and the hard work of building block clubs:

> We were taught to knock on doors and say, 'Let's get together with neighbors.' Some people would slam the door in our faces and some people would have us in for lunch. I'd go out on the street and think, 'Look at the horrible house at the end of the street. It must be a big problem.' Then you'd talk to people and they would say, 'The sidewalks are bad and the fire hydrants are broken.' When you'd ask about the house down the street, they would say, 'Yeah, that is a problem, but the fire hydrant in front of my house...'

Gruber added:

> You had to start out with what was the most immediate concern. Our second job was to nurture leadership. We didn't create leaders. All we would ever do is give people the opportunity to become the leader that was inside them all along.[4]

An example of this work can be seen in the individual block club reports compiled in a three year report written by Gruber.

> Ida, Crumb, Maud (Avenues): In August, 1977, thirty five people met with city safety officials about the problem with youth curfew violations. In October 1977, fifty people met with Community Development Dept. representatives to hear a description of the city's 3% Loan Program.
>
> Addison, Hecker, Schaeffer, East 71st: In 1977, this club was able to get a vacant house demolished, improved youth curfew enforcement, and a four-family house repaired. During the winter of 1977-78, the residents picketed a slum landlord's church in the suburbs after repeated attempts to gain his cooperation failed. This action jarred him into serious consideration of action on the group's demands.[5]

As with so many other organizations in Cleveland, St. Clair's most important issue was housing. It joined BWCC in fighting FHA over its foreclosure policies and its 518 (b) program that reimbursed home buyers for repairing defects in their houses that should have been caught by FHA inspectors.

The neighborhood not only faced problems with FHA and VA policies, but also with city policies dealing with open, vacant, and vandalized houses. SCSC did a survey of the neighborhood and found 141 vacant houses, many of which had been boarded up in a slipshod manner by the city.

Because the time was around Easter, St. Clair decided on a hit appropriate to the season. They arrived at the offices of the Community Development Department on Rockwell Ave. with a float featuring an Easter bunny and 141 Easter eggs, one for every vacant house in the neighborhood.

St. Clair's frustration with housing problems propelled it, along with groups such as Near West Neighbors in Action (NWNIA) and Citizens to Bring Broadway Back (CBBB), into leading the drive to create a housing court for Cleveland. Housing cases up to that time were handled on a rotating docket divided among the municipal court judges. Judges had no opportunity to develop an expertise on housing issues or to follow particular cases through the judicial process.

Kathy Jaksic, an activist and leader of St. Clair, described the campaign as one of educating and persuading the public and politicians that Cleveland needed a housing court. It was after the enabling legislation passed the state legislature that the campaign ran into its greatest opposition: from a municipal court that resented this invasion of its traditional jurisdiction.

St. Clair was one of the few groups to see real material benefit from the insurance redline fight. Like bank redlining, insurance redlining denied insurance to selected neighborhoods. Residents of neighborhoods denied insurance could not get mortgage financing or even auto insurance without paying exorbitant rates. Ending insurance redlining was a campaign that was otherwise considered a wash by other groups.

Through its research, St. Clair focused on one prime culprit, the Aetna Insurance Company, and targeted the company's insurance underwriting practices as part of a national campaign led by National People's Action (NPA). The campaign boxed Aetna in with enough damning evidence to finally compel a national agreement, establishing an Aetna-financed national fund for housing rehab to be shared by six cities, with Cleveland and, specifically, the St. Clair neighborhood as target areas. The financing provided by the Aetna settlement, resulted in formation of a non-profit housing corporation, COHAB.

COHAB's first house became an infamous albatross around COHAB's neck, and a harsh initial lesson in the hazards of the field, with problems with contractors and finding suitable homebuyers for the rehabbed house. However, it was successfully sold, and proved a valuable learning experience, in spite of all the tribulations it brought to the group.

Across town another organization was being started by two veterans of SCSC, Tom Gannon and Linda Hudecek. That organization was Citizens to Bring Broadway Back.

Citizens to Bring Broadway Back

Citizens to Bring Broadway Back (CBBB) started in the spring of 1977 when Joanne Roberts had her home insurance canceled because of inadequate water lines and fire protection in her neighborhood. Joanne had noticed the organizing going on in the Buckeye-Woodland neighborhood, and, with her sisters, began to contact friends and neighbors. In May 1977, they held an informal community meeting at the Boys' Club and drew a crowd of about 100 people. They turned to the Catholic Commission for assistance.

The assistance came in the form of Tom Gannon and organizer trainee Linda Hudecek, who met with Joanne Roberts and other leaders around Roberts's kitchen table. Gannon and Hudecek found a nucleus of residents who were passionate about saving their neighborhood and who had the time and energy to devote to the task.

What followed was a step-by-step lesson in how to establish a community organization. Hudecek and Gannon advised the group that it had to have an office and a paid staff to organize block clubs and its first convention. Hudecek was hired as a part-time organizer for what began as the Committee to Bring Broadway Back. Organizational help came not only from commission organizers, but also from veterans of an effort at organizing fifteen years earlier called The North Broadway Community Group, who formed an advisory group for the new committee and gave the group credibility in the neighborhood.

During the summer and fall of 1977, the group developed issues, started block clubs, won initial victories, held a neighborhood clean-up, and developed leadership. In February 1978, the group was incorporated, and in June, it received its 501(c) 3 status as a non-profit organization and a grant from the Gund Foundation. In July, it changed its name to Citizens to Bring Broadway Back to shed its ad hoc committee status. With funding secured and the organization legally established, CBBB held its first convention on October 14, 1978.

A number of issues shaped Citizens to Bring Broadway Back. One of the more unique issues was the Olympia Theatre.

The Olympia Theatre was a quality-of-life issue for the neighborhood. Residents remembered a time when their children could go to nearby stores or to the movies at the theatre without worrying about their safety. With the decline of the business district, there were fewer places than before for residents of any age to go to.

The final straw was when the Olympia Theatre on Broadway began to show adult films. For neighborhood residents, it was the final humiliation. Denise Gordeev, a leader of CBBB, spoke of the neighborhood's reaction:

> This was a beautiful neighborhood. We had the grocery, the bank, the bowling alley, everything you needed within walking distance. Whatever the problem, the show [the Olympia Theatre] wasn't making enough money, and the show was closed. Then they opened up and put the porno in there. Of all things, a porno place in a neighborhood like ours! This is a religious area. It's bad enough we do all this work, and we have this thrown in our faces.[7]

Adding insult to injury was the identity of the owner of the Olympia. Tom Olivio was considered one of the worst slumlords in the Broadway area, with almost 20 properties, none of which were up to code. The residents of Broadway were his victims twice over. First, he helped destroy the community through his real estate practices, then he assaulted the values of the neighborhood by bringing in an adult theater.

The issue caught many of Broadway's staff and leadership unaware of the intensity of local feelings about the issue. Paul Buccino of University Settlement House was at first skeptical:

> I went to a meeting where people felt degraded by this. When I went to join the picket line, I saw that, gee, they really cared about this issue. Then it became important. When you get people out there, it doesn't matter what the issue is.[8]

Daily demonstrations began in March 1981 to shut down the Olympia. Customers not only had to run a gantlet in front of the theater, but CBBB activists took pictures of them as they entered. None of the cameras had film, but it was an effective means of harassment.

The demonstrations escalated and targeted Olivio's home in the affluent suburb of University Heights. Another action was to picket the headquarters of the Laborers' Union where Tom Olivio's son, Dominic, was a business agent. Olivio retaliated by filing suit against CBBB for more than $5 million for harassment. The Catholic Commission provided legal defense, and the suit was dismissed.

Within a month, the Olympia Theatre went out of the adult film business. Olivio sold the building to a group of investors. With the help of CBBB and Broadway Area Housing Coalition (BAHC), it was redeveloped for apartments, offices, and commercial storefronts.

Union Miles Community Coalition

As Broadway was winning its first victories, groundwork was being laid for the founding of another of the major community organizations, the Union Miles Community Coalition (UMCC).

The roots of Union Miles were in two parent organizations, the Union Area Concerned Citizens and the Miles Area Congress, that merged after more than two years of working together.

Hugh Kidd, an early leader in local organizing, lived on Gibson Avenue and had started talking with his neighbors about common problems, such as low water pressure, stray dogs, and vacant houses. Then an organizer for one of the groups, Ken Esposito, came by hoping to organize a block club. Kidd described turning talk into action, and action into organization:

> Ken Esposito started to visit. He was looking to do some organiz-
> ing in the street, in the neighborhood. As we started to complain
> about these kinds of things, he said, 'Well, have you ever decided
> to come together as a street club and do something about it? It's
> very easy to get the city to come and snake out the storm sewers or
> clean the basements on the street.' We had never thought of that,
> but we came together and we did that, and it worked effectively.

Kidd and his neighbors recognized the need to band together with other street clubs:

> As we started to talk about it, there seemed to be a need to have
> more than just a street club. That's how we started to talk about
> forming a group to work through a lot of the problems that seemed
> to not only be a problem for Gibson, but for Anderson, Bentham,
> East 103 Street, and a number of the streets in that area. [9]

Esposito was surprised at the receptivity of the neighborhood. Residents were primed and ready to form block clubs and work on issues. Esposito gave several reasons for this. First, the residents were working class and lower-middle-class African-Americans who had moved into the area after it had been block-busted in the previous decade.

It was not a poor neighborhood, and it did not present the monumental difficulties that occur in organizing the poor. These people were homeowners, expecting to receive city services and prepared to do something about it if they didn't. The area also had just escaped having the I-490 innerbelt extension pushed through it. Residents had ferociously resisted the proposed throughway, and had gained organizational experience through successfully battling it.[10]

The groups became active on housing issues. The usual culprits were active in destroying the housing stock of the neighborhood: bank and insurance redlining, lack of money to finance home maintenance, racial discrimination. What set Union Miles off from the rest was that the biggest culprit of all was the federal government: not the Federal Home Administration (FHA), as in Buckeye-Woodland, but the Veterans Administration (VA).

The neighborhood had been hit with massive foreclosures of VA-insured houses. The campaign in Union Miles aimed to embarrass the VA into taking action on the problem. Organizer and future director of Union Miles, Marita Kavalec, described the campaign:

> Somehow, it seemed to have an impact, some sort of special significance to the community. These eyesores and safety hazards were there because of the VA. People automatically equated the VA with housing opportunities for those who had served their country...

Research revealed VA mismanagement of the properties on which it had foreclosed. Properties were not maintained, sat vacant for months, and were not effectively marketed. Kavalec described what happened when Union Miles invited a representative of the VA to tour the neighborhood to see the problems in person:

> We had hundreds of people waiting for him. Some of the guys came in their military attire. We really played it up so that the government military thing was there. Somehow, we were able to find a jeep, a real, true military jeep. One of the things we did was to take this guy on a tour to point out where the houses were, and he rode in this jeep with these American flags. We got a police escort to go around with him. The committee decided to serve him dinner in one of the vacant houses, rations or something for dinner.[11]

Besides being great fun and seizing media attention, the campaign met its goal for at least a while. Properties were cleaned up or boarded up and realtors were contacted to market them. Properties were turned over faster, as they hadn't in the past.

Early on, the Miles Area Congress and the Union Area Concerned Citizens began to work closely together. The final merger that created the Union Miles Community Coalition was a formality for what had already existed. The groups shared office space, initially at the offices of BWCC. They worked together on the same issues, and visitors could not tell their staffs apart. Furthermore, the very boundaries and names of the two groups were arbitrary, and did not reflect how residents looked upon their neighborhood.

Union Miles Community Coalition (UMCC) finally came together in 1979. By this time, it had become one of the leading organizations in the National People's Action (NPA) network on VA housing abuses. It was also second only to BWCC in confronting the issue of redlining. It was heavily involved in the organizing against Standard Oil of Ohio (SOHIO). UMCC merged with its spinoff development corporation, the Union Miles Development Corporation (UMDC) in 1985; however, the organizing ethos of UMCC continued to live on in the Union Miles Development Corporation, whose bylaws mandated an organizing program.

Near West Neighbors in Action

Near West Neighbors in Action (NWNIA) did not develop under the tutelage of the Catholic Commission. It began as the Ohio City Block Club Association (OCBCA) in 1977, in one of the most organized, contentious, diverse neighborhoods in Cleveland. The neighborhood included Puerto Ricans, Appalachians, African-Americans, young urban professionals restoring Victorian homes and retail spaces, and survivors of the left and counterculture of the 1960s. The neighborhood previously had undergone organizing by Dorothy Day's Catholic Workers movement, and the Communist Party had been active in the area. Gus Hall, its long-time leader, had lived in the neighborhood. Students for a Democratic Society (SDS) had organized in the area in the mid-1960s through the Education Research and Action Program (ERAP). Welfare rights organizing took place in the area, and an early rival of the commission groups, Active Clevelanders Together (ACT), had organized in the area and was fading from the scene as OCBCA was getting started.

Ohio City Block Club Association was formed from an uneasy alliance between newcomers who were renovating old houses in the neighborhood and poorer residents and the descendants of the political and cultural activism of the previous decade, who championed the interests of poorer residents. Polarization of the neighborhood was reflected in how residents referred to their neighborhood. Renovators called it "Ohio City". Their rivals called it "the Near West Side". Signs installed at entrances to the neighborhood by the city announcing the boundaries of Ohio City were defaced to read "Chic City". A popular poster displayed by the Near West Side partisans read, "Cleveland is an Ohio city. This is a neighborhood."

One of the founding block clubs of the Ohio City Block Club Association was begun on Carroll Avenue. It began to campaign against truck traffic and pollution from a local moving company. Tom Wagner, described the problem:

> These enormous moving vans ... would come in from all over the country or wherever they moved people, sit on Carroll Avenue, and idle their engines until dawn. This was really bad because in the wintertime, it was noisy. In the summertime, it was noisy and smelly. We didn't think they ought to be able to do that on a residential street. So Carroll Avenue's first block club issue was an attempt to get them to change their practice.[12]

The block club visited the zoning commission and other agencies downtown. The moving company was ordered out of the area, and left.

The defining issue in the neighborhood was arson. The epicenter of arson in Cleveland was the Near West Side neighborhood. The neighborhood is composed for the most part of small frame "workmen's cottages" built during the early part of the twentieth century when Cleveland was a manufacturing boomtown. What made arson so terrifying in this neighborhood was that houses were packed in so closely that, in many areas, neighbors could shake hands by reaching out of their side windows. Any large vacant lot usually meant that a house had burned down along with the houses on either side.

The Carroll Avenue block club waged one of the earliest campaigns against arson. At the time, the area that is now the track field of St. Ignatius High School was packed with buildings, including apartment buildings, an old brewery, and small frame houses. St. Ignatius had quietly acquired most of the property in anticipation of building the track field. The high school drew fire from the block club for not securing the properties that it had acquired. The predictable result was a series of terrifying fires that threatened the lives and property of the Carroll Avenue residents living just across a narrow street from the fires.

The block club confronted St. Ignatius with two demands. First, that the houses it had purchased be secured and maintained until they were demolished to prevent arson. The second was to level with the community about its development plans.

St. Ignatius boarded up and secured its vacant properties and began to change its attitude about the neighborhood. Wagner said: "I think they began to realize that the neighborhood was not something that was to be ignored. They could not appear to be an entity that was opposed to the local residents."[13]

Arson was symptomatic of the problems that plagued neighborhoods such as the Near West Side. Redlining and disinvestment led to the deterioration of housing, which resulted in foreclosures in which the financial institutions did not monitor the condition of the foreclosed property, or the outright abandonment of houses by landlords who simply walked away from them. The result were "OVV" houses: open, vacant, and vandalized structures that were prime targets for arson.

Arson was motivated in part by racial fears that a vacant house might be rented or purchased by Puerto Rican or African-American families. Arson was a profitable undertaking for unscrupulous landlords who wanted to collect insurance money. The usual thinking was that arson of multifamily buildings was for profit, and arson of single-family or two-family homes was motivated by thrill seekers or people motivated by racial prejudice or grudges against the targeted property owners or tenants. The extent of the problem was described in an early history of NWNIA written by Peggy Drury, a Catholic nun, in July 1980:

> The fire department believes that the Near West Side has been the target for most arsons for profit in the late 1970s. About 25% of the arson crimes in Cleveland took place in three wards in the Near West Side. This area is the focus because of deteriorating buildings that can be bought cheaply and insured for more than they are worth.[14]

The history documented one eleven day period in which fifty-five arson fires hit the Near West Side. Between April 1 and December 31, 1979, 100 units of housing were torched in just one ward of the neighborhood.

The Cleveland Press, in a January 15, 1979, article by Tony Natale, described the activities of three landlords active on the Near West Side. One landlord mentioned in the January 1979 Cleveland Press article was Joe Nader.

Nader became the poster child and arch villain of the anti-arson campaign launched by Near West Neighbors in Action (NWNIA). He owned a grocery on Scranton Road and fifty-four other properties throughout the west side. The Cleveland Fire Department stated that those properties had had forty suspicious fires in the 1970s when Nader was active. The Ohio Fair Plan, a state insurer of last resort, became suspicious of Nader's activities and complained to the FBI, which launched an investigation.

Near West Neighbors in Action declared Nader slumlord of the year and went to his house with a huge papier-mâché boot coming down on a firebug emblazoned with the logo "Help Stamp Out Arson!" to present the award. Nader was not at home, and the delegation was run off the property by his wife who, ironically, threw a boot at them!

The FBI investigation showed a pattern of over-insured buildings that were then the sites of suspicious fires. Arsonists hired by Nader testified to being ordered to torch two of his houses, one of which was burned twice to make sure the job was done. Tenants stated that Nader had jacked up the rent in one building in order to clear them out so it would be empty. Nader's former workmen testified that he had told them to make only the most cosmetic repairs because the building would soon be burned. Finally, Nader was convicted of trying to bribe a city inspector. That sent him to prison.

Near West Neighbors raised reward money and set up a tip line through which suspected arsonists could be turned in. Near West Neighbors in Action helped obtain grants that funded Project Secure. Project Secure boarded up vacant buildings in the neighborhood, using Community Development Block Grant (CDBG) money. They lobbied the city safety department to beef up the arson unit of the Cleveland police department and to put more investigators on the street to solve arson crimes.

Securing a mobile arson investigation lab was the crusade of Lenny Strimpel, who lived in the neighborhood of St. Coleman's parish near West 65th Street. Strimpel had long been zealous in fighting arson in his neighborhood, and had acquired a wealth of information about the details of arson incidents, who might be behind them, and what the neighborhood could do to fight the problem. Near West, along with other groups in the nearby Tremont and the Broadway areas lobbied city hall for a mobile arson unit, and the city finally purchased one for the fire department.

One casualty of the polarization that was always beneath the surface on the Near West Side was the Ohio City Block Club Association as a name and as an alliance between competing factions.

A flash point was a proposal to use Community Development Block Grant (CDBG) money to close off streets and install ersatz gaslights. The Near West Side partisans hit the roof. It represented to them all the snobbery of Ohio City, particularly the idea of CDBG money being spent on gaslights when there were so many unmet needs in the neighborhood. The proposal met its swift demise.

The dynamic of the issue continued into the 1979 convention of the Ohio City Block Club Association. By the time the convention closed, OCBCA had passed into history and Near West Neighbors In Action was born. The name represented both the victory of the Near West Side partisans and a focus on a militant activism much more in line with the overall movement in Cleveland.

Organizing the Organizations

The Cleveland groups were supported in their work by a number of organizations: National People's Action, the Center for Community Change, the Catholic Commission, and the Gund Foundation.

One of the most important organizations was the Ohio Action Training Center, better known as the Ohio Training Center. Its goal was to provide the groups with their own training center and a common strategic forum that was not restricted by the priorities of the larger institutions that had been so influential in the movement's start. It was to prove to be a daunting task.

The Ohio Training Center

The Ohio Training Center (OTC) was an attempt to replace the Catholic Commission as the institutional organizer of Cleveland's community groups. The name of the center was changed early in its existence to the Ohio Action Training

Center when it was discovered that the same name was being used by another organization. (Both names were commonly used during the time. For the convenience of the reader, the author will use Ohio Training Center)

The guiding presence behind the center was Joe Mariano, former head organizer of the Buckeye Woodland Community Congress, and later a trainer at the Catholic Commission. Mariano remembers how OTC began:

> I saw an opportunity around the state to do something. At that time (Bishop) Hickey was leaving for Washington, DC; and (Bishop) Pilla was coming in. Harry (Fagan) said, 'Things are going to change. Pilla is more into control.' I said to Harry, 'We've got to talk about spinning this thing off or there is going to be hell to pay.'[15]

The training center was not only a response to changes in the top of the diocese, it also reflected the growing restlessness of many organizers with the overbearing dominance of Fagan and a desire for a truly autonomous training center that could serve not only the Cleveland groups, but the entire state.

Dan Berry of the Gund Foundation, which funded the center, felt it held promise in raising the level of sophistication of the neighborhood groups. He described that promise:

> (It) was supposed to help the groups move to the next phase of what it means once you got the community's attention. OTC was supposed to be working with the groups to help them develop that next generation of community organizing strategies. I think it had built into it the notion (that) we need to develop more negotiating skills and all that underlies.[16]

On November 19, 1979, Fagan wrote to Doll detailing the premise that was to guide the Training & Technical Assistance (T&TA) program for 1980. Often, such letters are much more valuable than the founding proposals in explaining the thinking at the Catholic Commission. Doll thought the T&TA program merited special attention from his colleagues at Gund because the Gund archives contain at least a dozen copies of this letter.

Despite being one of the reasons that Mariano wanted to found the center, Fagan ends the letter with a strong statement in support of the Ohio Training Center as the future and hope of the commission in carrying on its work in community organizing. Fagan also saw a need to put some distance between the groups and the powerful diocese:

> While the Catholic Diocese has provided us with 'institutional

cover', it has produced a few constraints The tensions between the probability of future technical and financial resources and the eventual neighborhood autonomy of this program need to be seriously explored. To this exploratory end, we have begun the Ohio Training Center as an outgrowth of our neighborhood training and technical assistance program.[17]

Fagan also recognized the inherent tensions between the priorities of the organizing groups and the new development corporations rising to prominence. He wrote:

Realizing the attractiveness of physical development and housing rehabilitation programs, OTC has provided technical assistance to these organizations in order to insure that the 'people development' component and the 'neighborhood development' component coexist and complement, rather than conflict with each other. Too often in the past, we have watched staff and leadership energies totally usurped by a brand new development program.[18]

The Ohio Training Center (OTC) never really succeeded in fulfilling the hopes of the Catholic Commission. Probably the first blow that hit the OTC was the departure of Mariano, who followed his wife Karen Nielson to Chicago, where she had found a new organizing job. Most projects, such as the center, require the presence of a strong founding director or leader to launch it. Mariano left in 1981. Replacing him was George Barany, formerly of BWCC and, most recently, from the Senior Citizens Coalition.

While Ohio Training Center worked on developing issues, training organizers, and building coalitions, it never seemed to win the same loyalty from the groups as the old Catholic Commission and NPA had done. It should have easily claimed that loyalty. The staff at OTC were experienced organizers, well known to their peers. The center, according to veteran organizer Frank Ford, was essential in helping develop campaigns that otherwise would not have happened. Mike O'Brien, a long-time activist and board member of Near West Neighbors In Action, felt it played an irreplaceable role as a forum for the groups to come together to discuss strategies, issues, and future work.

But many groups were suspicious of the center. Their discontent was fueled by the failings of the SOHIO campaign to fight deregulation of natural gas in the early 1980s. Another problem was the passage of time. Acting as a coordinating body in the early 1980s was not as easy as it has been in the days of Project Interface and the founding of the groups. OTC found itself in the same crosshairs as Fagan had been.

The end of Ohio Training Center came in the campaign against Standard Oil of

Ohio (SOHIO), to be covered later. The OTC became the whipping boy for all the weaknesses of the campaign. Especially in the aftermath of a demonstration at the Chagrin Valley Hunt Club, everything came apart for the center. Its funding was cut, and by the summer of 1983 it was out of business.

The Cultures of Organizing in Cleveland

At first glance, the community organizations of this era appear almost identical. Most had been started with the help of the Catholic Commission. Many shared the same founding organizers. The start-up money for your group probably came from the Campaign for Human Development. The manual on getting the community group up and running was the same one that had launched BWCC. Groups went to the annual National People's Action convention in Washington, DC, and everyone had a different story to tell about Shel Trapp.

Underneath the veneer of unity were diverse neighborhoods with equally diverse organizations representing them. We will now turn to what united and divided the groups, and how they developed their own unique cultures of organizing within the broader unity.

Points of Unity

Whether you visited Buckeye Woodland Community Congress, or Near West Neighbors in Action, you could expect to find the same general characteristics.

- An aversion to politics

The most common reason given for the groups' aversion to politics, was their 501(c) 3 tax status, but the real reasons behind their refusal to become involved in politics ran deeper.

There are many ways to become involved in politics. Legalistic niceties, such as a tax status, are routinely and continuously sidestepped or subverted in the real world. Holding leadership and staff positions in 501(c) 3 organizations did not stop a Who's Who of neighborhood luminaries from openly supporting Mike White in his successful 1989 campaign for mayor. Tax status is a convenient excuse, not a convincing explanation.

A more compelling reason was the groups' desire to maintain their independence and credibility in communities that looked upon politics and politicians with withering cynicism. Shel Trapp said that the attitude of National People's Action towards politicians was that, "you may be our friend today, but tomorrow is another day." Remaining independent of politics gave the groups the ability to use city hall as a target for their campaigns.

The goal of the groups was for residents of the neighborhood to run their community from the grassroots. This was in complete contrast to the dynamics of electing a candidate who uses their power to serve the constituency. It was a clash between direct and representative democracy.

The groups also had to work constantly to maintain at least a show of unity within neighborhoods fragmented by class, race, ethnicity, religion, and politics. To take political stands or to develop a political arm of the neighborhood movement would have dried up any support at city hall, raised the ire of the supporting foundations, and divided the neighborhoods further. Another example of this caution was how the groups avoided any stand on the issue of school busing to desegregate Cleveland schools.

• The One True Church: National People's Action

If any national organization could claim to have had the organizing franchise in Cleveland, it was National People's Action (NPA) and its education and research arm, the National Training and Information Center (NTIC). With the exception of Citizen Action, which really occupied an entirely different niche, no other organizing network or organizer training center had a presence in Cleveland. As Ann Pratt of Union Miles said: "Different training center! Are you kidding? That'd be like Pat Robertson going to seek help from the Buddha!"

NPA provided the fledgling groups with a vast store of organizing experience from which to draw. NPA got its start working on the same set of issues in Chicago that were central to the Cleveland groups: housing, redlining, destructive federal policies, insensitive and unresponsive local governments. In Shel Trapp, NTIC's lead organizer, the staff of the groups found their hero. In NPA leader Gail Cincotta, the rank and file and leadership found a hero who shared their background and values, and who had come from a community similar to theirs.

The annual NPA convention in Washington, D.C., was an opportunity for leaders and staffs to network, exchange information about their local organizing, and get an overview of national campaigns. In addition, the convention featured a combined hit on some targeted institution or agency in the nation's capitol.

Gail Long, former director of Merrick House, whose involvement in neighborhood issues began in the mid-1960s, felt that the Catholic Commission organizers, under the tutelage of NPA, were better trained than any previous class of organizers. The groups knew how to produce leaders who would otherwise have never been found. Basic skills for running meetings, setting agendas and strategic thinking also were developed. [21] On certain issues, such as Community Reinvestment Act (CRA) organizing, their contribution was beyond dispute.

The downside was a rigid, dogmatic style of organizing that made alliances and coalitions with other groups difficult, if not impossible, and narrowed the range of issues on which the groups would work. The NPA groups had the answer, period. No other viewpoints were solicited. George Barany was critical of NPA for its lack of democracy, its domination by Gail Cincotta, and its lack of training opportunities in development for leaders.

• Direct action

All of the groups confronted their opponents with direct-action tactics of demonstrations and civil disobedience. This style had its origins in National People's Action. According to Trapp, what distinguished NPA from other organizing networks was its willingness to use direct action. NPA's maxim was, "If you aren't ready to fight, you aren't ready to win." [22]

The Cleveland groups differed widely on their willingness to "hit" their foes. Some groups, such as Buckeye, positively gloried in using these tactics; other groups used them only when all else failed. For the targets of these hits, it was never a pleasant experience, but it always got their attention. The best description of direct action as used by the groups was provided by George Barany:

> We would send a letter to invite an official out. If the official didn't respond, you'd take a group of people down to his office, uninvited. If the official sent a letter and said I'm sorry I can't come, you took a group of people down to his office and made him respond, right then and there. If the official responded and said he was sending a representative, the first attempt over the phone was to negotiate: No representative, you come yourself. But, ultimately, if the representative came and if the representative said at any point during the meeting, I can't answer that; I don't have the authority, that representative was thrown out of the meeting. We'd say: 'You've wasted people's time here, we don't have time to waste. We asked for someone in authority to come. We're sorry that you came, but you now have to leave.' Right then and there, an action would be planned for either that evening, depending on the issue, depending on how much work had been done on that issue, in a sense, what level it was, because we certainly weren't above taking people to some official's house in the evening to confront him over the lack of responsiveness. That was our style, to force people to the negotiating table so that negotiations would be serious. [23]

Points of Division

There were differences between organizations and organizers in how they operated within the larger unity. The differences fell into different traditions and cultures of organizing.

• The Buckeye Tradition

Buckeye Woodland Community Congress (BWCC), Union Miles Community Coalition (UMCC), and the Senior Citizens Coalition (SCC) and, especially BWCC, helped blaze the trail in community organizing in Cleveland. They inspired the formation of other organizations and supplied valuable information on how to get started, select issues, and develop leaders. People who were with these groups or who had passed through them in their careers were the organizing establishment in Cleveland.

The Buckeye tradition also gave community organizing in Cleveland its fierce reputation. There was an aura of braggadocio with these organizations, where the toughness of the leadership, the ability to "produce" bodies to an action or convention, and the militancy of tactics were a source of pride, and even arrogance. Other organizations in Cleveland compared themselves to the Buckeye tradition, both in what they admired and in what repelled them.

• The Broadway Tradition

Citizens to Bring Broadway Back (CBBB), and Southeast Clevelanders Together (SECT) were in this style. CBBB was a haven for those who were turned off by the machismo of other groups. One organizer who found refuge in CBBB was Judy Opalach, who was told by Joe Mariano that she wasn't mean enough to be an organizer when she worked for SCSC. They were willing to confront if driven to it, without turning it into a fetish. They were attracted to consensus-based decision making. They were more insular in their focus, but had a solid track record for working on citywide issues, as well.

The Broadway tradition was heavily influenced by the experience of many of the women from Broadway at the Seneca Peace Encampment in the early 1980s that protested against the deployment of Pershing missiles to Europe. The result was a critique of the super-macho, super-confrontational style of organizing prevalent at the time. Bobbi Reichtell of Broadway described this experience and its influence:

> The quality about the organizing that took place at the peace camp
> that was not prevalent in neighborhood organizing at the time was
> a sense of empowerment and self-directedness. The thing that was
> really impressive about the women's peace camp was that it was
> not a patriarchal system at all, but more egalitarian: building con-
> sensus, not the majority rule system. [24]

Reichtell soon realized that this learning experience clashed with the organizing status quo back in Cleveland:

> Coming back to Cleveland then, there was a lull where here we are
> and we're stuck in these patterns and ways of doing business,
> which has a very macho air to it. You know, throwing your weight
> around. It's almost no different than the people you are dealing
> with, with corporations and city hall. [25]

Those local organizers who went through the Seneca Peace Camp experience came to favor consensus-style decision-making. They developed new ways people could empower themselves, instead of being empowered by someone else. They came to look upon theirs as a feminist school of organizing. It was not welcomed by the organizing establishment of NPA. They came back to preach the word to an organizers' conference in Chicago, and were ridiculed by the male organizers.

• The Back-to-Basics Tradition

Near West Neighbors in Action (NWNIA), and St. Clair Superior Coalition (SCSC) represented this tradition which reacted against the heavy emphasis on big citywide and national issues. They felt that they had to concentrate their attention on neighborhood, block club issues, however important the larger issues might be. The main representatives of this tendency were Renee Berry and Kathy Jaksic (SCSC), Maggie Britton (Ohio Training Center, formerly SCSC), Gloria Aron, and Eileen Kelly (NWNIA). They felt that they had been burned and misadvised on such citywide issues as the Standard Oil of Ohio (SOHIO) campaign. They favored a back-to-basics approach that prioritized the unglamorous tasks of tackling everyday problems in their neighborhoods.

The most eloquent spokesperson for this was Eileen Kelly, who came to the staff of Near West during the summer of 1982, when such campaigns as natural gas deregulation and rising sewer rates were top priorities for many of the older organizers in the group. As a result of her experience with her block club on West 47th Street, Kelly felt that the issues, while perhaps important, did not resonate with the people she was working with. She said:

> I mean, there are hundreds of things you could involve people in, the things that were really affecting them and making them afraid, making them worry about their kids ...Those were the things immediately on their street, and each street was different. The fear in that neighborhood was huge at the time. People felt so helpless, and most people that were renters felt helpless because they were renters. Most people were on welfare. They felt hopeless because they had no money.

Issues such as sewer or gas rates did not resonate with the people on West 47th Street, according to Kelly, who continued:

> So you pay five dollars less on gas? That's not going to make a lot of difference, but if you get rid of that house next door that catches on fire every other night, that makes a lot of difference. [26]

The back-to-basics school gained credibility with the blowback from the SOHIO campaign. Kelly, as director, went so far as to win board approval to withdraw from citywide coalitions. After a very rough period of financial troubles, focusing on neighborhood issues stabilized NWNIA and extended its life as an organization.

A Movement Organized

By the close of 1979, the community organizing movement in Cleveland was an established, flourishing force in the city's neighborhoods. It had a cadre of experienced organizers who trained new organizers and consulted with new groups. The groups developed their own distinct identities and areas of expertise. Leaders from the block clubs and neighborhoods were, day by day and issue by issue, becoming more sophisticated, knowledgeable organizers in their own right. The movement had institutional cover, research resources, and fundraising aid from the Catholic Commission and the George Gund Foundation. Cleveland groups had sealed an alliance with National People's Action and other national organizations. They were in the national forefront of such issues as bank and insurance redlining, arson, the use of Community Development Block Grant money, and the reform of Veterans Administration and Federal Home Administration policies. The usual movers and shakers in Cleveland could no longer make policies for the neighborhoods by fiat. There was a new voice demanding to be heard: the voice of the organized neighborhoods of Cleveland.

Chapter 5

Pols and Activists

We were ... politically irrelevant.[1]

Mike O'Brien, *Near West Neighbors in Action* (NWNIA)

The environment that allowed the community organizations of Cleveland to exist was shaped by the politics of the time. The victories of the social movements of the 1960s were codified into laws, policies, and programs in the 1970s. Legislation passed in the 1970s, such as the Community Reinvestment Act and The Community Development Block Grant program, gave the groups tools and resources that were vital to their success and growth. The administration of President Jimmy Carter seemed to be in their corner with the sponsorship of the National Commission on Neighborhoods and the appointment of such neighborhood heroes as Monsignor Geno Baroni to a HUD position. Former antiwar activists, such as Sam Brown and Marge Tabakian, were put in charge of ACTION, the governing agency for Volunteers In Service To America (VISTA) and the Peace Corps. We will see how the arrival of the Reagan administration changed all the rules to the detriment of community organizing in Cleveland. Yet, for all of the importance of politics in their daily lives, the political realm was always a foreign and dangerous land for the groups. They were never able to fashion a coherent, believable, and effective political strategy. It was one of their major weaknesses.

Locally, the groups shared turf and frequently came into conflict with local politicians, especially city councilmembers. The conflict centered on one key question: Who represents the people of the neighborhood, or ward? The community organizations said, "We do." The local councilmember said, "I do." At one time, the conflict would be bitter. At another, the combatants would announce their enduring love and respect for one another.

The political attitudes of the community organizations were shaped by their status as 501(c)(3) non-profits that were required to be non-partisan. Even more important than this was how they saw their mission. Tom Gannon, of the Catholic Commission explained:

> We didn't want to get involved in partisan organizing because that would divide the community and would make people suspicious of what we were doing. We didn't want to get into anyone's political camp. We didn't want an organization that would politicize like some of the Model Cities organizations, where people were fighting for jobs and things like that. We wanted to develop that independent base so we could make the politicians accountable to us. [2]

One of the ways in which the conflict was expressed was when neighborhood residents came up against a particular problem. The old fashioned response was to call the councilmember to get it taken care of. The community organizing approach was to hold a meeting to discuss the issue, see how much support it had, then create a strategy for the group to call a city hall official or get a meeting with a city representative. Marlene Weslian of Citizens to Bring Broadway Back (CBBB) described their experience:

> At the time, one councilman was Joe Kowalski, who was really entrenched. He had been a councilman for a long time, and that was why when we went to meetings and people said, "Oh, we don't have to do anything. Let's just call Joe." We normally said "OK, fine, call Joe. If Joe does something, then that's terrific. Then we can move on to another issue and that's been taken care of." Nine times out of ten, of course, it didn't happen, and Joe didn't come through. [3]

According to Tom Wagner, who helped found the Ohio City Block Club Association (OCBCA) and Near West Neighbors In Action (NWNIA), the organizations even held an attitude that the councilmembers were not needed:

> There was a sense that...they worked for you and they were your employees and you told them what you wanted done. There was also that sense that you didn't need them. You could enact change in terms of the local level. In that sense, you were in competition with them. There was a clear sense in the upper echelon of community organizing in Cleveland at that time that you were in competition with the councilpersons as an agent of change. [4]

Most councilmembers greeted the new organizations with suspicion, fear and hostility. Certainly, one of the most dramatic examples of this was an incident in the Union Miles neighborhood.

Marita Kavalec of Union Miles Community Coalition (UMCC) was knocking on doors in the neighborhood, when she encountered a supporter of councilmember John Barnes:

> He cut the conversation short, went into another room, and came out with a shotgun. He escorted me out of the house, off the street to where my car was. Carrying his gun, he let it be known that I was in such-and-such a councilman's ward: John Barnes. This was John Barnes's territory, and I didn't have John Barnes's permission to be there. They would really appreciate it if I never showed up in that area again. If I did, he said there were going to be consequences. It was outrageous! [5]

In Union Miles, the other council member was Earl Turner, who would come to Union Miles street club meetings, make promises, and derail Union Miles Community Coalition's efforts to organize. To counter this, UMCC held "Earl Turner nights" when as many block clubs would meet as could be managed. Turner could not be everywhere at once, so most of the clubs could conduct their business in peace. [6]

The neighborhood with the most conflicted relationship was on the Near West Side between Near West Neighbors in Action and Helen Smith. Smith was no stranger to the organizing scene, and had been an activist and leader with the OCBCA before it became NWNIA. Her sister, Margery Knipe, was an early and much revered organizer with the Catholic Commission. Smith felt the other councilmembers were much more paranoid about the groups than she was. She described the situation:

> Well, coming out of an organizing effort I had a different perspective than a lot of the others there [did]. They looked on it as a major threat. I remember meetings where they were beating up on the bishop. We had a number of meetings with Bishop William Cosgrove and councilperson Mary Zone pounding on the table. Especially the older councilmen were not used to that type of organization. [7]

In spite of this familiarity, there was a great deal of conflict between Smith and Near West. Smith felt that Near West was not representative of the neighborhood, or was just representative of a marginal part of it. Feeding into the conflict were the ancient Near West Side conflicts between rehabbers and poor people and their advocates, a conflict in which Helen was labeled as the councilmember of the "Ohio City" (i.e., gentrifiers, yuppies, etc.) faction.

Chuck Ackerman, a longtime activist in the neighborhood, felt this depiction of Smith was inaccurate. She may have represented the rehabbers; however, she also had a base with long-time homeowners in the area who had little use for poor and minority residents and even less use for their defenders. Smith's ability to straddle this divide between yuppie newcomers and old-time residents was the reason for her political durability. [8]

At the same time, Smith was a realist who recognized the inevitability of Near West in its prime and waited for the final days of the group in the late 1980s before she pulled the plug on ward funds and delivered the coup de grace.

Eileen Kelly became an organizer and director of Near West in a time of transition. She had no part in earlier feuds and controversies. She described the complex relationship between Smith and NWNIA, especially in light of her continued financial support of the group:

> That $10,000 from her made the place stay open. Maybe she didn't
> think of it that way. We had board members calling her. We had
> Bob (Pollack, Director of Near West Housing Corporation) calling
> her. Helen is a strong woman. There was always trouble with
> Helen. She always had a different agenda than NWNIA [did]. [9]

In the competition between the community organizations and the councilmembers of the era, the clear winners were the local politicians. They had learned from their encounters with the groups. They realized that gains could be made by cooperating.

In the end, community organizations did not replace the power of the council members. Instead, a new type of ward machine that was more efficient and powerful than the classic machines of the past appeared on the scene: the non-profit development corporation that, in most cases, was a spinoff of the old organizing groups.

The development corporations founded to rehab housing, and promote economic development, were expensive. They were also far safer politically than the wild and woolly community organizations.

The council representatives had what the old advocacy groups did not: money to support staff and fund the programs of the new development corporations. The priorities of the development corporations and those of the councilmembers fit like a glove.

Community organizations not only dealt with councilmembers, they also dealt with mayors. The two most important mayors for the groups were Dennis Kucinich (1977-1979) and George Voinovich (1979-1989).

The relationship with Dennis Kucinich was particularly interesting because Kucinich and the groups used much of the same rhetoric and appealed to many of the same constituencies. Instead of cooperation, however, the relationship was combative and competitive, to the detriment of both parties.

At first look, the relationship between Kucinich and the groups should have been a love fest. Both claimed the banner of urban populism. Both claimed to represent the "little people" against the insensivity of big government and the rapaciousness of big business. They had the same enemies. Yet shared values, foes, and constituencies were not enough for them to make common cause.

The conflict was between two very different viewpoints on where power came from and the role of politicians in bringing about social change. Both sides were trapped by the narrowness of their perspectives. The resulting conflict set back the cause of progressive social change and reform in Cleveland for decades.

In his book on the Kucinich years, *The Crisis of Growth Politics*, Todd Swanstrom described how the relationship between Kucinich and the community groups was doomed from the start by their similarities.

> When Kucinich was elected mayor, he suddenly became, for the community groups, an ex officio member of the corporate elite. But Kucinich, of course, did not see himself this way. He saw himself as the head of a new citywide community organization, which would represent the neighborhoods in larger struggles against the banks and corporations.[10]

Swanstrom pointed to a revealing statement Kucinich made to the Plain Dealer early in his administration:

> 'Activist community groups are unnecessary with a mayor who understands their needs' Above all, Kucinich needed to be perceived as the initiator, as the one who delivered the goods, in order to solidify his electoral base.[11]

The groups were no less driven by their internal dynamics:

> The community groups could not afford to let Kucinich take credit for delivering all the benefits to the neighborhoods. Moreover, their tendency to personalize issues meant that whoever was in power was held responsible for the problems. Kucinich, therefore, was fair game.[12]

The relationship did not start off on a bad note. There was a honeymoon period. George Barany, who was an organizer at the time with Buckeye Woodland Community Congress (BWCC) remembered election night, when the staff and leadership of Buckeye waited to see if Kucinich would show up for a promised negotiating session:

We waited in that office to see if he would show up. At 10:30 at night, he showed up with his wife Sandy and the media and a small entourage, and we did have a negotiating session, brief, right then and there. We felt, this guy's great. We're going to get some real opportunities here.[13]

The honeymoon did not last very long. One of the first groups to come into conflict with the administration was Citizens to Bring Broadway Back (CBBB). An abandoned house in CBBB's area had been on the emergency demolition list of the city for two months. There had already been three arson fires at the house.

Facing the inaction of the city, Broadway decided to do the job for them and put together a neighborhood demolition crew that began demolishing the house. According to organizer Linda Hudecek, they soon changed their minds. It was the city's job to tear down the house. It was the city that had to be called to account. Hudecek recalled:

So we loaded all of this charred wood into this pickup truck and a couple of cars...and only about ten of us went down to Community Development...We went into the building carrying all this charred wood in, we're dropping ashes and junk everywhere, and she (Community Development Director Betty Grdina) started scream- ing, "Call the police, call the police," kicking us out, yelling, "Get these people out of my office; just get them out of here!" She was literally shoving people out of the office.[14]

The hit happened about one or two p.m. in the afternoon, and by four p.m. the house was demolished by the city. It was one of CBBB's first victories. It was also one of the first of its run-ins with the Kucinich administration.

The construction of a new fire station at East 49th Street and Broadway was one of the most important accomplishments of CBBB in its early years. The original firehouse serving the area was over 100 years old, and obsolete. The floors could not support the load of modern fire equipment. Original plans called for the new station to be constructed in 1975. The years rolled by, and still the promised fire station never materialized. This was not only a fire protection issue; it was also an issue of the politics of community development funding during the Kucinich administration.

Through a source at city hall that they named "Deep Throat" after the inform- ant in the Watergate scandal, Broadway learned that community development money had been set aside for the station. The official story was that it was gone. The goal of the new firehouse campaign of CBBB was to go after money that was there yet not there.

One of the more famous events in the campaign was a meeting scheduled with city Finance Director Joseph Tegreene to discuss the fire station issue. The meeting was set for October 27, 1978, close to Halloween. At the last minute, Tegreene canceled, and sent Frank Mancuso, a powerless underling, in his place.

In retrospect, the participants at the meeting felt sorry for Mancuso, who delivered a very simple message: He could not agree to anything. Because it was around Halloween, Paul Buccino from University Settlement House had dressed a pumpkin up to represent the mayor and tried to get answers from the pumpkin. There was no response from the pumpkin to any of Buccino's questions.

The meeting then adjourned to Community Development Director Betty Grdina's house to ask why the city was not responding after nine attempts to get the mayor to talk to Broadway. About ninety people reconvened the meeting in front of Grdina's Near West Side apartment, shouting to her to come down and meet with them. Police were called, and one officer finally agreed to deliver a letter from the group to Grdina.

Tom Gannon of the Catholic Commission, commented on the response to CBBB's visit to Grdina's apartment:

> They went to her house, and she called the police on them. The groups had gone to a lot of people's homes before that, but no one had ever called the police on them, not the Republican administration, not Ralph Perk. Now the 'people's mayor's' community development director had called the police on them. [16]

The confrontation with Kucinich was a risky proposition for Buccino, who was the executive director of the University Settlement House. The day after the demonstration in front of Grdina's apartment, Buccino received a call from Benny Bonnano, an ally of Kucinich's in city council, who wanted to know what was going on. Bonnano related that Kucinich's chief of staff, Bob Weissman, was furious over the hit. The administration had an opening to punish Buccino. A Community Development Block Grant to provide matching funds for the settlement house was pending. Furthermore, Buccino was in hot water with the head of the Neighborhood Centers Association (NCA), Bob Bond, who was not a fan of community organizing. Buccino was confronted with two tests. Would his agency be punished by the Kucinich administration? Was the independence of his agency within NCA real or theoretical? He passed on both counts. University Settlement received its CDBG money and, after a heated argument with Bond, the independence of Buccino's agency was maintained. [17]

Faced with situations such as these, activists had to be concerned not only with their impact on the position of the group with the city, but also within their communities. In the case of the action at Betty Grdina's apartment, it caused the departure of some older early supporters of the group. Linda Hudecek and Marlene Weslian thought the confrontational tactics did not fit their view of appropriate conduct before authority figures. There were ways you petitioned your government and ways you did not.

One of the lowest points in the relationship between the community groups and city hall, came at the November, 1978 Neighborhoods Conference. The conference represented ten groups, with about 700 people attending. Representing the city administration were Community Development Director Betty Grdina, Chief of Staff Bob Weissman, and Finance Director Joseph G. Tegreene.

The conflict was initiated by Betty Grdina's refusal to answer questions from the audience until the agenda was changed to include her colleagues, who were not scheduled to speak. Conference leaders finally allowed Weissman two minutes to speak, after which he was to be cut off.[18] Tom Gannon described what happened:

> [Weissman said], 'This is how you're going to have to behave if you want to come down to city hall and see us.' He started to read from a legal pad, and he went on for a few minutes and all of a sudden people said, 'What? What is this bullshit!', and they started saying, 'Sit down! Boo! You work for us! You work for us!' [19]

Diane Yambor of Buckeye took the microphone away from Weissman after telling him his time was up. He kept talking. Fanny Lewis, a Kucinich supporter and future councilmember, marched up on stage and a struggle for the microphone began between Lewis and Agnes Jackson of BWCC. Gannon described what happened next:

> Fanny Lewis walked up and hit Agnes Jackson over the head with the microphone. You heard this big "bong" go over the PA system. Sarah Turner (of BWCC) picked up a chair and was going to hit Fanny over the back of the head with the chair, at which point one of the organizers took the chair away, and Sarah grabbed another one, and that's when all hell broke loose. [20]

According to Diane Yambor, the last they saw of the mayor's delegation that night was them running from the hall, although no one was chasing them.

In response, Weissman cut off city hall cooperation with Buckeye Woodland Community Congrss, Citizens to Bring Broadway Back, and the St. Clair Superior Coalition. "We're going to cut these groups off. They are off limits." Weissman said. "We can maintain our contacts with the neighborhoods by dealing with other groups in those areas."[21] He also attacked Harry Fagan and the Catholic Commission for employing "professional agitators and organizers."

Diane Yambor speculated that the groups sponsoring the conference had been set up by Grdina's insistence that Weissman be allowed to talk when the conference had really wanted to learn from her why the city had blocked an investigation by HUD of CDBG spending, especially when the investigation would have dealt, for the most part, with the actions of preceding administrations. Bernice Krumhansl of

SCSC also speculated that Grdina's actions were an effort to dodge the CDBG issue. Harry Fagan thought the reason was more basic than that: "Weissman came (to the conference) to lecture, not to listen. He found out he was dealing with grownups who don't get lectured to."

Conflicts between Kucinich and the groups were also reflected within particular neighborhoods. This was especially true in the St.Clair-Superior neighborhood. Only the Near West Side was as diverse, cantankerous, and contentious as the St. Clair Superior neighborhood was. Everything was complicated, with maddeningly complex ethnic, racial, and political dynamics. Adding to the volatile mix was the socialization of the populace to the bare-knuckles school of ward and union politics. Forbearance, tolerance, and a willingness to forgive and forget were conspicuously absent from these traditions. [22]

Kucinich used his alliance with Tanya Grdina, his safety director, and Betty Grdina to build a power base in the neighborhood. The Grdina family was a powerful presence in the neighborhood. Immigrants from Slovenia, they established themselves commercially in the neighborhood early in the century. The streetcars would stop in front of their store and immigrants new to the country would find lodging, jobs and other services provided by people who spoke their language and were familiar with their culture.

Kucinich challenged St. Clair, which he regarded as a rival. According to Swanstrom, he was also angered by the refusal by the coalition to help him defeat the recall election in August 1978. The word on the streets was that if people had a problem, they should call Kucinich, not the coalition. The coalition became alarmed by the Kucinich campaign creating separate leaflets for white and black areas, as one of the main goals of the coalition was to avoid racial conflict in the neighborhood.

The confrontation at the neighborhoods conference not only led to a formal break with the Kucinich administration, it also split St. Clair. Nine coalition board members resigned, citing too much power in the hands of the president Bernice Krumhansl, the domination of organizers who were pushing "grandiose" issues not important to neighborhood residents, lack of financial accountability, and staff being composed of outsiders who did not understand the neighborhood. Krumhansl responded that the loyalty of those who resigned was to Kucinich, not to the neighborhood. [23] Those who resigned said they were going to found a rival organization, but nothing ever came of it.

While the board resignations were dramatic, they were not unexpected, and St. Clair loyalists were already organizing to recruit new members and limit the damage. Ron Jaksic, relative of coalition leader Kathy Jaksic and an officer of SCSC, described the damage:

> My view then was it took away any innocence, any virginity the
> coalition had in terms of good representational leadership. It
> knocked it out, killed it, made it difficult to be as broad based. [24]

The conflict even split families, such as the Jaksic family for instance:

> We had plenty of family arguments with my one aunt. She was old ward club, old guard kind of leadership in the Perry Home organization, [which] was formed years ago, more of a social group. At the time, [it was] a group that was concerned with integration. It was more racist in the sense of preserving the area from change.[25]

Nothing ever was simple in St. Clair. As Ron Jaksic remembered:

> So it was really twisted. Every component in St. Clair was not a straight shot. It made for a very frustrating period of time. I think that affected a lot of leadership, burnt out a lot of people.[26]

The controversy between St. Clair Superior Coalition and the Kucinich administration moved from about who did what to whom at the neighborhoods conference to the issue of a blocked housing program. The controversy was public, with major opinion pieces authored by both sides appearing in the "Forum" page of the *Plain Dealer*.

St. Clair Superior Coalition was putting together a housing rehab program for the neighborhood, and it wanted HUD to approve funds to hire an outside consultant: a community organization from San Francisco.

The China Town Corporation had succeeded in starting a housing rehab program. Their experience, the coalition felt, was relevant to the situation St. Clair Superior Coalition was facing. According to Ron Jaksic, Kucinich activists began a rumor campaign claiming the San Francisco group and SCSC were preparing for a Chinese takeover of the neighborhood. SCSC even tried to do an end run around the administration to appeal directly to HUD for grant approval, something that HUD never looked upon with favor. The Kucinich administration vetoed SCSC's funding request.

In December 1978, Buckeye Woodland Community Congress and other Cleveland groups proposed to the National Commission on Neighborhoods that Community Development Block Grant (CDBG) funds be directly funneled to neighborhood organizations to make sure that something got down to the neighborhood level. This flew in the face of the history of the CDBG program. The CDBG program had been designed to give local governments and politicians some say over how federal dollars were spent. It was a reaction to the experience with War on Poverty programs in which federal dollars funded the opposition to many city halls, with predictable backlash from local politicians. BWCC's request was simply not going to happen.

The administration responded to its neighborhood critics in a May 26, 1979, "Forum" article in the *Plain Dealer* written by Betty Grdina.

First, Grdina cited a long list of neighborhood accomplishments. Then she stated that plenty of neighborhood groups had no problem with city hall. The problem, she wrote, was with a minority of groups who were addicted to the media spotlight and to confrontation politics. Grdina did not mention the master's thesis the mayor had written on confrontation politics or the fact that he was a skilled practitioner of the art, as well.

She outlined the administration's position on the groups: The foundations and charities were front groups in corporate Cleveland's war on Kucinich:

> Their motives can be traced to the elite foundations which control funding to these groups: the Cleveland Foundation, the Gund Foundation, and even the Catholic Commission on Community Action, a branch of the Catholic Charities Appeal, which donates substantial sums and trains organizers in the use of confrontation tactics.
>
> Even Republic Steel is involved in the attempt to subvert a neighborhood group. The Growth Association is now showing interest in neighborhood groups. Believe it or not, Cleveland Trust's Brock Weir has also come out 'in favor' of neighborhood groups.[27]

Grdina also stated that the groups had set themselves up as unelected representatives of the neighborhoods. She cited largess from the Kucinich administration for the St. Clair-Superior area, and charged that the leaders of the SCSC also had political ambitions. She discussed the housing issue, and stated that there was no need to hire an outside consultant. She defended the dissident groups in the SCSC area, saying they are being ignored by the media and silenced by SCSC. Next, she leveled her ire at the organizers by accusing them of creating media events that distorted the picture of what was really going on in the neighborhoods. Grdina charged the organizers with inciting "Ku Klux Klan" style intimidation of public officials such as CBBB's bringing arson debris to her office and the demonstration in front of her residence.

She finally leveled the classic accusation used by anyone who is the target of dissent. She played the "outside agitators" card:

> The organizers claim they choose disruptive, and sometimes violent methods because that's the only way to get results for the neighborhoods. But many of the organizers have never lived in the neighborhoods they claim to represent. They are only visiting. They will move to try to 'organize' other areas when they have finished trying to wreck St.Clair Superior's reputation.[28]

Grdina ended her piece:

> The ultimate question is their right to speak for the neighborhoods at all, since they are funded by corporate contributions and run by nonresident organizers.[29]

In the battle of the "Forum" pages, it was now the turn of the SCSC to respond to the Kucinich administration. The response came in a June 11, 1979, Forum article titled "The Coalition Speaks." Written by Bernice Krumhansl and Rev. Thomas Martin, a leader of the coalition, it related the history of the organization and its willingness to work with all institutions that affected the neighborhood. They then cited various issues they worked on and all the accomplishments of SCSC.

Krumhansl and Martin then responded directly to Grdina. First, they asked if SCSC was so insignificant, why it was being attacked. Then they described their recent convention with 340 delegates, forty-five block clubs, and fifty-five streets represented. What other organization in the neighborhood could claim the same diversity and inclusiveness? They added that they were not into confrontation for the sake of confrontation, but only in those cases where they were being ignored.

In discussing the neighborhoods conference, Krumhansl and Martin charged that one person was knocked to the ground by a Kucinich aide and that St. Clair opposed the rudeness shown Weissman. They charged that SCSC was being singled out for punishment, and rejected out of hand the charge they were a partisan organization, saying no one was prevented from participating on the basis of his or her political affiliation.

St. Clair gave its view of the controversy over bringing in representatives of the San Francisco group as consultants. Grdina had charged that there was no need for the San Francisco group's studies. Grdina said that the San Francisco group could not contribute anything because they did not know Cleveland. SCSC responded that the Chinatown group was from a neighborhood similar to St. Clair-Superior and that SCSC felt it could learn from them. Finally, Grdina said she felt the HUD technical assistance grant was a waste of the taxpayers' money. That was true, SCSC said. Because of city hall opposition, the money had been given to another city.[30]

Significantly, the coalition response did not mention, and did not even attempt to answer probably one of the most cutting charges of the Kucinich administration, that they were front groups for corporate power in its battle with Kucinich. Ron Jaksic commented on this:

> Foundations give you parameters. They don't dictate specific activities. Coalition groups were not going to be told what to do unless it was something they wanted. It was so far fetched. They were fighting some of the same corporations in different ways at different times [as the Kucinich administration was].[31]

Kucinich finally became so exasperated with the groups that he asked for a meeting with Bishop James Hickey of the Cleveland Catholic Diocese to complain about the Catholic Commission's involvement with groups that were in conflict with him. In the highly polarized world of Cleveland politics during the Kucinich era, the Catholic Commission was under suspicion by all. At the start of the Kucinich administration, his opponents criticized the groups for making Kucinich look good, and giving him de facto support. Now, the groups were looked upon by Kucinich as being in an unholy alliance with the banks and corporations in an effort to destroy his administration.

At the time, Kucinich was stonewalling a number of community groups on issues around which they were organizing. Kucinich's feeler to the Catholic Commission began with a call to commission director Harry Fagan.

Kucinich asked him to meet him at Tony's Diner, a place he had popularized during his administration. Fagan refused the invitation, saying that he did not speak for the neighborhood groups. Kucinich called Bishop Hickey, who, with Kucinich on hold, called Fagan and told him "The mayor is on the phone and he said you won't meet with him." Fagan agreed to meet at the diocesan offices with the mayor and the bishop, at the bishop's request. Reverend Ed Camille, another staff person at the Catholic Commission, was also a part of the meeting. Fagan told the Bishop what Kucinich was going to say: that the commission was sponsoring paid outside agitators and added, "Ed (Camille), you take the 'paid' part. Bishop, you take the outsider part, and I'll take 'the agitators'."

True to his prediction, the meeting took place, and Kucinich leveled the expected accusations. Rev. Camille said the mayor had to be kidding about paid agitators. The organizers worked for miserable salaries that could best be called stipends. The bishop said, "Outsiders? Well, I'm an outsider. I came here from a college in Rome." Fagan finished by saying that the only agitator he was aware of was in his wife's washing machine. The meeting ended.

The next day, Kucinich announced that the Citizens to Bring Broadway Back neighborhood would get its fire station and other demands would be met, as well. But Kucinich never forgave Fagan, and the rift between the groups and his administration became permanent.[32]

There were many different explanations on what went wrong with relations between the groups and the Kucinich administration. On one level, the organizations found the demeanor of the functionaries of the administration intolerably arrogant. As George Barany of BWCC said, "These people came in with a head of steam, and we as organizers thought we were arrogant. They put us to shame." Kucinich was blamed for setting the tone of the administration, but most of the organizers and leaders of the community groups focused their wrath on his staff members, particularly Bob Weissman.

Beneath the issue of Kucinich's staff, was the central issue of who would control the neighborhood agenda and who really represented the interests of the residents of Cleveland's neighborhoods. Tom Gannon stated, "They had a mentality that once they were elected, they were the sole representatives of the people."

Gannon said that after the brawl at the 1978 Neighborhoods Conference, that attitude became clear. "I think what they had said was that the community groups were not controlled by them, could not be controlled by them, and if they couldn't be controlled by them, then they should be destroyed or silenced. I think that it was their paranoid attitude, and [their] need to control."[34] Kathy Jaksic of SCSC commented on the central issue in her neighborhood in the Kucinich era: "I think it was a question of authority. Who was going to decide for this neighborhood?"[35]

Many people feel that the Kucinich era was a historic opportunity that was lost forever. Frank Ford, who worked for the Ohio Training Center and who went on to become director of Union Miles Development Corporation (UMDC), commented on these missed opportunities to build a powerful urban populist movement from the grassroots to city hall.

> I mean, he was handed a gift. A progressive mayor in any town, anywhere today, just think how they would have loved to have been in a town where there was that kind of neighborhood organizing. This town had more neighborhood organizing, more potential grassroots, low-income power than maybe any other city in the country. He didn't know how to use that.[36]

A consensus of veterans of the era is that Mayor George Voinovich (1980-1988) was the beneficiary from Kucinich's disastrous relationship with the neighborhood groups. Tom Gannon described the difference:

> George Voinovich would come out and say, 'You guys are a real pain in the ass, but I'm glad you're here. I'm glad because you're doing good things for the neighborhood, and we all want to do good things for the neighborhood. Even though you drive me crazy and give me a hard time, I'm sincere, and you're sincere, so we are all one big happy family.'[37]

What was critical on the part of the neighborhood groups during the Voinovich era was a feeling that they were recognized and respected and would be listened to by a city administration, regardless what their other disappointments and disagreements with the administration might be.

There were a number of reasons for Voinovich's positive relationship with the neighborhood groups. First, Voinovich did not dwell in the same Manichean world as the Kucinich administration had. He recognized that there were not only friends and enemies, but also innocent civilians.

Voinovich was also a Republican in an overwhelmingly Democratic town. A fondness for confrontation politics would have been suicidal. As committed to Republican politics as he was, he was not a Reaganite, and was continuously going to Washington to plead the case of the cities before the Reagan Revolution. An example was his endorsement of the activities surrounding Reclaim America Week in 1982. Reclaim America Week, which was a rolling protest against the policies and priorities of the Reagan Revolution, was hardly a campaign designed to warm the hearts of traditional Republicans.

Further, Voinovich was not seen as the supreme political power broker of Cleveland politics during the 1980s. That title, along with all the credit and blame, fell to only one man, City Council President George Forbes. Cleveland during this period was akin to a constitutional monarchy, with Voinovich as the kindly and beloved king and Forbes as the despised, but effective prime minister. Voinovich could afford to be popular, thanks to George Forbes.

The environment that greeted community organizations when they began in the 1970s was different from the one that characterized the Voinovich years. During the Perk and Kucinich years, the community groups were fighting for recognition, respect, and some minimal responsiveness from city hall. They were met with fear, contempt, and intransigence.

By the time Voinovich came into office, city hall, was starting to learn its lessons on how to deal with the groups. Councilmembers and bureaucrats started to realize that they might gain from giving group representatives the time of day, and might gain some good will in the wards as well. City hall began to get used to a political environment that included organized neighborhood groups.

This is not to say the Voinovich era was a love fest, and there were no conflicts. There was plenty of conflict in the fight over community development funding on the Near West Side. Another example was Union Miles Community Coalition (UMCC) "hitting" the mayor at the airport with a demonstration, resulting in the mayor lecturing them on proper conduct but not exiling them from city hall as Bob Weissman had done.

The groups had changed the rules for city hall in dealing with the neighborhoods. City government became more responsive, and this change undermined confrontation tactics that were a hallmark of the groups. Their lightning was not stolen; it was denied a clear target. With the founding of the neighborhood development corporations, neighborhood groups became less the voice of grassroots democracy, and more the providers of services for neighborhoods and for councilmembers. The groups were incorporated into the same municipal system they had previously besieged.

The community groups and Mayor Voinovich were also on different time lines. Voinovich was just starting in his career as mayor. The groups, while vigorous on the surface and full of the old fire and arrogance, were terminally ill.

One source of institutional and financial support after another was drying up or pulling back. The Hickey administration of the Cleveland Catholic Diocese was ending. Harry Fagan was packing his bags. Major sources of funding and support from the federal government were ending with the advent of the Reagan era. Foundation support was either headed for new pastures or was getting increasingly nervous about the tactics of the community groups.

The focus of the neighborhood groups also changed with the prominence of such issues as SOHIO. Their targets were no longer located at city hall. There was less of a chance for the Voinovich administration to come into conflict with the groups than there had been with Perk or Kucinich.

What Voinovich gave these groups was something few others had offered: respect. For the analysts of public policy who tally the scores of who won and who lost on a particular issue, this may not calculate. However, respect means the world for organizations that represent people who have always been ignored, discounted, and disrespected. The appearance of respect, above all else, may have been the key to Voinovich's peace with the groups.

Part 2:

Campaigns

Chapter 6

THE BATTLE AGAINST REDLINING

Barb Pertz of the Buckeye Woodland Community Congress was on her way to a meeting of the Federal Home Loan Board when her flight was delayed in Cleveland due to snow. She decided to kill some time by posing as a wife whose husband was being transferred to Cleveland. She asked for advice from an airport realtor about looking for homes in the Buckeye area.

> I said, 'Oh, OK, what about this area?', which was the Buckeye Woodland area. She said to me, 'Oh, you wouldn't want to live there.' 'Why?' 'Blacks are moving in.' 'Oh really?' 'Yeah.'[1]

Pertz thanked her for the information, then made a simple request:

> I said, 'I know you are going to think I'm crazy, but would you do it in red so I could be sure, absolutely sure, that this is not the area we want to live in?' She said, 'Sure,' and took a red pencil and literally redlined my neighborhood. I folded up the map very nicely and thanked her. Then I proceeded to the Federal Home Loan Board and took out the map. I said, 'You can't even get in or out of the city of Cleveland without being redlined!'[2]

The Pre-CRA Era

Redlining, the practice of denying financial or insurance services based on geography, was explored in a paper written by Rev. Dan Reidy, titled *Greenlining: Reinvestment Strategies to Save Our Urban Housing*. Published by the Catholic

73

Commission in December of 1974, it was the first published document to discuss possible strategies to deal with redlining in the Cleveland area.

Reidy began his paper by reviewing the extent of disinvestment and housing abandonment nationally and locally. He cited massive abandonment of housing in Cleveland in the early 1970s. He analyzed how redlining worked, using examples from other cities, and then focused on Cleveland.

Cleveland's largest bank, the Cleveland Trust Company, with seventy two per cent of its branches in the city, wrote only twenty four per cent of its mortgages in the city. Some financial institutions, such as Central National Bank and Third Federal Savings & Loan, had better records. Others, such as Shaker Savings, only wrote mortgages that were government-insured, showing minimal confidence in the city.[3]

Reidy proposed a three-part strategy for fighting disinvestment focused on community organizing, neighborhood housing services, and new legal and legislative measures.

Community organizing had three main features: researching issues, using disinvestment issues to unite diverse communities, and organizing to pressure lending institutions. Research gathered ammunition, and targeted particularly egregious cases of redlining. Tactics were discussed, such as transfer pledges, where the campaign would sign up customers of particular lenders who would pledge to pull their money from those lenders if they did not negotiate with community groups to change their practices.

The Neighborhood Housing Services (NHS) program was another suggestion. Modeled on a Pittsburgh project and promoted by the federal government, it acted in concert with lenders to stimulate reinvestment in target neighborhoods. NHSs created a high-risk loan pool with local lenders to start lending based on the qualifications of the applicant, not the location of the property. Reidy had mixed feelings about this model. NHS only showed interest in areas with strong community organizations and housing stock, not in weaker, harder hit neighborhoods.[4]

Reidy then laid out the possible legal recourses, mostly through recently passed civil rights legislation and court rulings. At best, these remedies were long shots. With local legislation, the paper discussed moves by local governments, such as City of Chicago, to link city deposits with lenders with records for lending in the neighborhoods and to recommend similar legislation in Cleveland.

Another contributor documenting the problem of redlining was a Case Western Reserve University student, Ruth Ann O'Leary. She interned with the Catholic Commission and went on to work for the City Planning Commission under Director Norm Krumholz.

O'Leary developed the methodology for documenting redlining, and her work was used to train organizers and leaders on the issue. *You Can Bet on It: Redlining in Cleveland* used both 1974 data and the 1970 census to document redlining in Cleveland. The study was submitted to the Congress of the United States as evidence for the need for the passage of the Community Reinvestment Act (CRA). The study also identified two local institutions that would become targets of the groups in their redlining organizing: Cleveland Trust, and Central National Bank.

One of the earliest efforts to combat redling, and one that used some of the strategies promoted in Reidy's *Greenlining* study, was begun by Active Clevelanders Together (ACT). ACT was an organization only loosely allied with the Catholic Commission. Its territory was the west side of Cleveland, and it initially was sponsored by the United Church of Christ. ACT operated in a pre-CRA environment, and was going after the savings and loans of the west side instead of the major banks that would be the target of later organizing.

John Calkins, the organizer for ACT, came upon a central theme of the campaign while interviewing a representative of the St. Rocco church credit union on Cleveland's west side. The representative asked Calkins to do some homework: First, go to the savings and loans in the city and count the number of tellers they had compared to the number of mortgage loan officers. Then go to their suburban branches and count again.

Calkins found that the inner city branches had far more tellers than mortgage loan officers, and the suburban branches had the opposite: more mortgage loan officers than tellers. The explanation was simple. In the city, you had older homeowners who had paid off their mortgages and were sitting on thousands of dollars of savings. In the suburbs, you had young home buyers, who had few savings and low equity in their houses. The money from the city was subsidizing the suburbs.[5] O'Leary made a similar point in her study: that redlining in the city was used to stimulate housing demand in the suburbs.[6]

ACT's strategy of attack had several parts. The first part was an intensive investigation into the lending activities of the savings and loans. In the time before the Home Mortgage Disclosure Act (HMDA), that meant days spent down at the county administration building going over records of mortgage transactions on the Near West Side, which was the target neighborhood of the campaign.

The second part of the strategy was a greenlining campaign, a door-to-door effort to solicit pledges from neighborhood residents to withdraw their savings from savings and loans that did not invest in the neighborhood. This not only provided a club to hold over the heads of the lending institutions, but it was an excellent way to recruit people and to give them an investment in the campaign.

The third part of the strategy was to go after the heads of the offending institutions, face to face, to get them to the bargaining table. At this time, in the mid-1970s, the savings and loans were largely family owned. There were real people who lived in the area for the community groups to go after, in contrast to later years, when mergers and purchases of lending institutions made those who pulled the strings far less accessible. ACT went after board members and searched for anything they could use as leverage in local churches investing in these institutions.[7]

The initial target was Ohio Savings and Loan Association, followed by Cardinal

Federal Savings and Loan, Cleveland Federal, People's Savings and Loan, and Third Federal, Broadview and Lincoln Savings and Loan.[8] ACT used the greenlining strategy of threatening savings and loans with the withdrawal of customer accounts, in a massive door-to-door effort that collected 500 pledge cards promising to withdraw $750,000 from Ohio Savings.

ACT demanded that the savings and loans open their books so that ACT could see the ratio between savings in the city and lending in the suburbs. ACT also demanded that there would be a one-for-one ratio of lending and savings in the city: that for every dollar in savings in the city, there be a dollar in lending in the city. No savings and loan companies took ACT up on the offer. They merely volunteered to participate in the Neighborhood Housing Services (NHS) program on the Near West Side.

The effort did result in some investment in the neighborhoods. According to Joe Garcia, then director of the West Side Community House, the existence of Neighborhood Housing Services on the Near West Side was a direct result of the disinvestment organizing that ACT championed. He did not think ACT got much credit for its work.[9]

In a 1976 article in the *Plain Dealer*, ACT took credit for a 134% increase in mortgage and home improvement loans on the Near West Side. The savings and loans maintained that it had been a very good year for their industry.

Garcia considered the campaign waged by ACT against the history of the savings and loan scandals of the 1980s. The excuse that savings and loans in Cleveland constantly made when confronted by the demands of groups such as ACT was that investing in inner city neighborhoods presented an unacceptable risk because of social and economic realities in those neighborhoods. Then the same industry threw caution to the wind in the 1980s, resulting in one of the greatest financial meltdowns in U.S. history. Garcia wondered what could have been done if the money lost in that catastrophe had been invested in America's urban neighborhoods. He said we would be living in a different and much better country today.[10]

FHA/VA Issues

While ACT took on redlining directly with the savings and loan industry, other groups were introduced to the issue through campaigns targeting FHA and VA housing policies. The link between redlining and FHA/VA policies was a major point of Reidy's greenlining study. Other studies added to the mounting pile of evidence. One of the first studies was *The Impact of Foreclosures on Government Insured Mortgages in the Cleveland Area* by Janice Cogger of the Cleveland's city planning commission in July 1977. The study described the high rate of foreclosures of government insured mortgages in Cleveland to a tune of almost 700 foreclosures per year since 1973.

The problem was not only the high number of foreclosures, but their location on the east side of Cleveland in areas experiencing racial transition. Among these neighborhoods were the Buckeye-Woodland and Union-Miles communities. At ground zero for these foreclosures were large, low-income families who were desperate for housing and who found themselves shut out of the regular rental market and ignored by government housing programs. In particular, the Section 8 program was irrelevant to their housing needs because it only constructed or rehabbed one and two-bedroom apartments.

Cogger concluded that the foreclosure policies of the FHA and VA subverted other efforts to provide housing to those in need and to stabilize neighborhoods:

> While expanding housing opportunities for low and moderate-income families and improving neighborhood conditions are ostensibly important objective(s) of federal and local policy, the problems associated with foreclosure may be more significant in undermining these objectives than such programs as Section 8, NHS, and Community Development Revenue Sharing are in advancing them. [11]

This suggested a radical policy proposal. Cogger proposed more intensive pre-foreclosure counseling for those in trouble, plus a policy of not foreclosing in those cases where families can pay at least twenty five per cent of their monthly income towards their mortgage. She wrote:

> We are not nearly so concerned with the possibility that some individuals might shirk their mortgage responsibilities as we are with the reality that hundreds, if not thousands of families who lack the resources needed to (buy) adequate housing are being displaced from their homes...each year by foreclosure. [12]

Taking the discussion further, Cleveland State University student and future organizer Linda Hudecek examined redlining in the St. Clair-Superior neighborhood in a March 1977 paper titled *Disinvestment in the St.Clair Superior Community: Indications of Redlining*. The study found the existence of a dual home financing system in the neighborhood and discussed how FHA and VA-insured mortgages contributed to redlining and real estate speculation. Hudecek described the difference between conventional and government-subsidized mortgage markets:

> Two separate housing markets exist in the St.Clair-Superior Community.... the two different markets consist of 1) conventional financing with small sum mortgages, large down payments, short maturities, and under appraised purchase prices; 2) government insured financing with large sum mortgages, small down payments, long range maturities and equal appraisals and assessments. Thus, the conclusion can be drawn that government insured mortgages are financing the normal flow of the housing market. [13]

Hudecek showed how this dual system operated to finance real estate speculation, where the goal is to buy cheap and sell dear.

> For example, a particular parcel on East 79th Street has an assessed value of $13,596.00. It was bought on 2-5-76 for $6,000.00 with a $4,000.00 mortgage. It was resold 9 months later for $15,000.00 with a VA mortgage for the same amount.[14]

Hudecek summarized her findings:

> Not only has the initial decision to redline detrimentally affected the neighborhood, but persistent patterns of land speculation, coupled with increased reliance on government insured mortgages only abet the devaluation of property. Unfortunately FHA and VA financed properties bring with them high rates of foreclosure, and thus increased instances of vacancies. Ultimately the combination of non-availability of conventional moneys and the disadvantages of FHA/VA financing produce a housing stock that decreases monthly in property value.[15]

O'Leary also wrote of the perversion of the original mission of the FHA/VA programs:

> With the risk of investment assumed by the government, these institutions have pirated the true intent of the program from that of enabling lower-income people to get involved in home ownership to one of luring people who can't really afford a mortgage and home maintenance costs into a program that enriches the middlemen.[16]

The Buckeye Woodland Community Congress made FHA practices an early focus of its organizing. The campaign centered around two issues. The first was the practice of mortgage companies and real estate companies who financed houses through FHA for people who had no business buying a house. When they failed to make payments, foreclosure soon followed, and FHA paid off the mortgage company. The house would be sold again through FHA, and the cycle continued. One particular house changed hands eight times in a short period of time. Each transaction brought profit for the realtor and to the mortgage company. Karen Nielson, organizer for BWCC, described the process:

> We started documenting that there were mortgage companies and real estate companies in cahoots. We tried to trace realtors selling a house that wasn't in good shape to someone who needed a mort-

gage and later realized that it needed a new furnace. The mortgage company would foreclose and get paid off, then finance it to the next homeowner who came through. [17]

Nielson told one story that became legendary among activists in Cleveland working on the issue:

> One family who just moved to Cleveland, [and who] had three kids, had gone to a realtor to find a place to rent. The realtor said, 'Why don't you buy?' They said, 'We're new to the city. We need to get established.' The realtor said, 'I see you have a nice car out there. I'll take the tires as down payment.' That's how they got their house. Well, they got into it and it was the roof or the furnace that went. Those stories were repeated over and over again. [18]

Buckeye Woodland Community Congress made arrangements for Lutheran Housing Corporation to begin foreclosure counseling for people caught in the revolving door of FHA foreclosures; however, the campaign was impeded by the attitudes of those victimized, and the general community. The victims were ashamed of what had happened to them, and the general community felt that the families had gotten themselves in trouble by not being careful in their business dealings.

The other FHA issue dealt with the condition of the properties. The general assumption among people in the community was that FHA had inspected and approved the houses. The assumption was wrong. All sorts of problems with FHA houses were described. One house had a crack running through the exterior wall so large you could see outside through it. One victim of the shoddy standards of FHA inspections was Sarah Turner, a domestic who became one of the future leaders of BWCC. Nielson described Turner as a natural leader for the campaign:

> She was very up-front, had some righteous anger, and loved preaching. She'd get up and talk about her eight kids. She bought this house. There was not even a sink in the bathroom. They had to brush their teeth in the tub. The foundation was separating in the basement. She was the epitome of someone who had been sucked in by a realtor. [19]

Turner took her story to the community:

> Sarah stood up at the meeting and started talking about her house. People started saying, 'That happened to me, too.' People realized that it wasn't an individual problem but the whole community. That galvanized people. [20]

The campaign demanded that the 518-(b) program be made available to those who had been victimized in purchasing dilapidated FHA properties. The 518-(b) program was designed to compensate property owners who had purchased FHA houses between 1968 and 1973. The program was supposed to either reimburse people for repairs that were needed on houses that had been given a clean bill of health by inspectors or replace houses that were too far gone, which is what happened in Turner's case. The local HUD office was no help, and BWCC made frequent "hits" on the local office. The campaign was both local, and national, with a series of National People's Action hits against HUD headquarters in Washington DC. It was a long campaign, stretching from 1975 until 1980. Nielson described its successes:

> It was some long, hard fight. We had inspectors out, HUD officials, tours, the whole bit. Sarah Turner got a new house. HUD said it would take too much money to bring it (the old house) up to code. We went after the city to put more heat on HUD. I know that countless homeowners got big money.[21]

The CRA Era

The redlining issue was revolutionized by the passage of the Home Mortgage Disclosure Act (HMDA) in 1974 and the Community Reinvestment Act (CRA) in 1977. The HMDA required financial institutions to document their lending activities. The Community Reinvestment Act required financial institutions to serve the credit needs of the communities they did business in. Organizations could now easily access information on lending practices of financial institutions and take action against those who were redlining neighborhoods.

Buckeye began educating the community about CRA and how to use it. The process began with a meeting held at Benedictine High School that asked the 150 people in attendance one simple question. What could be done for the neighborhood if you had a million dollars? The participants proposed mortgage loans, rehab loans, and economic development funding. A list of demands came out of the meeting that became BWCC's platform for the coming fight for reinvestment in the neighborhood.[22]

Local banks were invited to discuss their receptivity to the demands. The Cleveland Trust Company became a special target, with its several branches in the neighborhood, a large amount of savings from the neighborhood residents, and very little loan money coming back into the area.

In one of the early attempted meetings with the bank, Gene DiSimone, branch manager of the Buckeye office, stood up representatives from BWCC in early February 1979, who had previously delivered a list of credit needs to him. One of the worst mistakes a targeted institution could make with a community organization, especially a community organization such as BWCC, was to fail to show up for a meeting.

The next night, three vans and forty members of Buckeye showed up at DiSimone's apartment building and gained access to his building, but he did not answer his door. BWCC proceeded to canvass his neighbors; they got into the newspapers, publicized their grievances, and fired the opening salvo against the Cleveland Trust Co, which continued to stonewall BWCC over the next year.

In May 1979, the bank, soon to be renamed Ameritrust, applied to the Federal Reserve Bank for permission to merge with three subsidiaries in Lorain, Painsville, and Columbus and to take over a bank in Cincinnati. BWCC saw an opportunity to get the bank's attention. It filed a formal challenge to the proposed merger.

The challenge not only was a major organizing effort, it was also a challenging technical and educational effort. No manuals were available to tell groups how to challenge a merger. The regulations had not even been written. But Buckeye was not alone. The research arm of National People's Action, the National Training and Information Center (NTIC), and the Center for Community Change in Washington, DC, helped. Housing lawyer Peter Ishkin from the Cleveland Legal Aid Society also helped. Otherwise, Buckeye was left to write the book on CRA challenges in Cleveland. [23]

One reason for the conflict between Buckeye and Cleveland Trust was the CEO of Cleveland Trust, M. Brock Weir. Weir was an executive officer of the old school who did not recognize the right of community organizations to influence how his company conducted its business. Tough, abrasive, and arrogant, he was among the most formidable foes Buckeye ever faced. Pat Kinney, lead organizer on the CRA issue, felt that Weir personalized all his conflicts into tests of will. One example of this was his war with Mayor Dennis Kucinich during Cleveland's financial default.

Buckeye leader Sharon Bryant called Weir a thorn in the side of BWCC and related how, on one occasion, he derided BWCC's membership, calling them "porch monkeys". Bryant said, "I thought if I could face Brock Weir in a certain situation, I would have no problem dealing with Central [National Bank] or Society [for Savings] or National City [Bank], or any other bank because I'd dealt with him." [24]

One of the more interesting documents in the archives of the BWCC is a memo from Jerry Jarrett, president of Cleveland Trust, to M. Brock Weir about the bank's stance in the community. In it, Jarrett states the need for the company to have good relations with the community and located the neighborhood group's initiative in the context of declining public sector funding for neighborhoods.

> Against this background, it is not sufficient to advise any group that 'our record is good', or 'we comply with the law,' or 'we don't discriminate in lending,' or 'if you satisfy our criteria, you'll get a loan.' These positions do not address the current attitudes of the community groups or present the Cleveland Trust Company's case in an affirmative and meaningful posture. [25]

He cited the examples of community involvement used to defend Cleveland Trust's record. Jarrett acknowledged the value of such involvement, but noted that it was contingent upon the initiative of local branch managers and it was not backed by the full organizational commitment of the bank. He wrote:

> What is needed is a program involving (a) counseling with neighborhood communities as to both the individual and group level on credit availability, private and federal credit programs, methods of obtaining credit, and responsibilities of obtaining credit; and (b) the development by the bank of profitable community credit programs meeting acceptable credit standards; to be offered to individuals and groups utilizing either private and/or federal funds. [26]

Jarrett ended the memo with a proposal to put Cleveland Trust's CRA officer in the branch administration office to work with branches on the issues. Underlined in the BWCC copy is the proposal that "the Community Reinvestment Officer shall have overall responsibility for development, implementation and coordination of profitable community credit programs..." [27]

No record remains of the fate of Jarrett's recommendations, but the memo makes several interesting points. First, it was made on March 23, 1979, early in the escalation of the conflict between BWCC and Cleveland Trust. Second, it implies some internal dissent with Weir's confrontational style.

Buckeye's challenge to Cleveland Trust dragged on through the summer. In the view of Pat Kinney, a lead organizer on the issue, the big hold up was that the federal government was unfamiliar with the regulations and was split between wanting to get the two parties negotiating or rejecting the merger. Furthermore, the Federal Reserve Bank as an institution is dedicated to keeping the banking industry happy and to serving its needs, not to challenging its decisions. BWCC ended up organizing against the Federal Reserve Bank to get it to reach a decision. One goal was to get the Federal Reserve Bank to sponsor a public meeting on its challenge. The result was a five-hour meeting on August 22, 1979.

The meeting, held at Buckeye's headquarters, detailed Buckeye's complaint against Cleveland Trust. BWCC leader Sharon Bryant said that the neighborhood had been raped by banking institutions such as Cleveland Trust. Another BWCC leader, Diane Yambor, presented evidence from the Home Mortgage Disclosure Act reports for 1977 that Cleveland Trust had taken in $74 million from its two Buckeye area branches, but had lent out only $210,000. It presented affidavits from seven community residents, who had been denied loans by Cleveland Trust, although other lenders later approved them. Finally, they denounced discriminatory application procedures that left no records of applications being taken. A loan officer for the bank wrote loan application information on a legal pad, then threw the sheets away once the loan had been denied. [28]

One of the best summations of Buckeye's frustration with the Federal Reserve

Bank is a document it submitted in reply to the November 13, 1979 report issued by the Federal Reserve Bank stating preliminary findings in the Cleveland Trust case and pointing toward an approval of the merger.

Buckeye believed that the Federal Reserve was not even following its own guidelines for assessing CRA compliance. In a document the BWCC filed for a December 12, 1979 meeting, the Federal Reserve Bank has replaced Cleveland Trust as the target of the group's scorn and criticism. BWCC was accustomed to beating up bureaucrats. The December 12 document opened with BWCC lecturing the Federal Reserve Bank as it would a dense student: "We request at this time that the staff members from the FRB of Cleveland take notes from the beginning because we would rather not go through this case a third time for you!"[29]

Buckeye outlined the requirements of what bank examiners were supposed to consider and which the group felt the Federal Reserve Bank ignored and cited official CRA statements and communications with Cleveland Trust. It documented instances when Cleveland Trust had ignored them, avoided meetings, and stonewalled them. Some of the most scathing criticisms were of the bank examiners who had allowed Cleveland Trust to define its community as Cuyahoga County and submitted a road map of the county. The document reasoned:

> In plain, simple language, CRA was not established because banks
> have redlined the suburbs! They have not redlined Cuyahoga
> County as a whole! Nor have they redlined their "Entire
> Community!" ...The problem only exists in low and moderate-
> income neighborhoods. Therefore, local communities must be
> identified and analyzed separately.[30]

Another complaint about the bank's report was how Cleveland Trust's obligations to reach out to the community had been ignored by the bank examiners. BWCC argued that Federal Reserve officials took Cleveland Trust's word for its outreach efforts with minimal fact checking.

> We would like the record to show that the Cleveland Trust
> Company at no time contacted any of the following members of our
> community regarding credit needs: 1) No PTAs, 2) No religious
> organizations, 3) No block clubs, 4) No neighborhood organiza-
> tions, 5) No coalitions of neighborhood organizations, 6) No
> minorities, 7) No non-profit housing development corporations.[31]

The meetings for which Cleveland Trust took credit were those in which they stood up BWCC after repeated communications and reminders from the group. The aborted meeting with DiSimone was particularly galling for BWCC. It complained:

> Our CRA committee went back to Mr. DeSimone's office the fol-
> lowing day and questioned him on his absence. He responded by

stating, 'It's not my fault. I was instructed by downtown not to attend.' [32]

Buckeye even caught Cleveland Trust in a lie about its meeting with the Union Miles Community Coalition:

> The report states the Cleveland Trust Company met with the Union Miles Coalition to determine their credit needs. At this time, we would like the record to show that statement is totally incorrect. We would like to present as evidence a notarized affidavit from the president of the Union Miles Coalition verifying that at no time has a meeting between Cleveland Trust and the Union Miles Coalition taken place. [33]

Buckeye continued laying out its position with complaints about Cleveland Trust's failure to locally advertise and market its services, and contrasts the bank's inaction, with that of the State Savings and Loan Company. It describes Cleveland Trust's failure to offer credit counseling or to contact Lutheran Housing Corporation to use its expertise in credit counseling, and it concluded that Cleveland Trust had not pursued business with local companies or with the residential mortgage market, contenting itself with simply providing brochures and literature at its branches. Buckeye concluded:

> BWCC wants the record to show that the Cleveland Trust Company refuses to use local advertising for the purpose of encouraging potential loan applicant(s) from our neighborhood. The bank refuses to use financial counseling programs to promote mortgage applicants in our neighborhood. Finally, the bank refuses to use its loan and branch personnel to promote potential housing-related loans in the Buckeye Woodland neighborhood. [34]

One requirement of the CRA regulations was that financial institutions' boards of directors must be informed of and involved in CRA requirements. BWCC cited a visit it had made to a bank director who was also chancellor of Case Western Reserve University to ask him about Cleveland Trust's behavior in June 1979. He responded that he did not know why they were in his office, and directed them to go to other board members and leave him alone.

Buckeye suggested that his response was indicative of how uninvolved board members were, and accused:

> Now as far as the FRB (Federal Reserve Bank) of Cleveland and the Public Report that was published, we can conclude that the examiners never inquired to the extent of the board of directors' participation in this issue. The examiners portrayed the same bla-

tant ignorance for the CRA and for the procedures as do the chairman and board of directors of the Cleveland Trust Company![35]

Buckeye turned to the issue of branch offices in low and moderate-income neighborhoods. They noted again that the examiners were supposed to evaluate the bank on this topic, and that they had ignored the information. Over the past four years, Cleveland Trust had eliminated branches in two low-income neighborhoods while expanding in ten new suburban communities. At the rate Cleveland Trust was going, they would, over the next fifty years, pull out of all the low-income communities and eighty five percent of the City of Cleveland. [36]

Buckeye examined Cleveland Trust's listing of the community organizations with which it said it had developed relationships. Two groups were unknown. Four other organizations, the Lakewood Community Development Corporation, Forest Hills Church Housing Corporation, the Heights Area Project, Jewish Community Federation, and the East Cleveland Community Development Corporation, were not even in Cleveland, and only the East Cleveland Community Development Corporation served a low-income population.

Buckeye took particular note of Cleveland Trust's listing of Lutheran Housing Corporation (LHC) as an example of its community involvement. True, Lutheran Housing had had a loan with Cleveland Trust, but no generosity was shown the corporation by the bank. BWCC related a community meeting in which it had asked Cleveland Trust for favorable financing rates for Lutheran. Dell Duncan, the bank official, responded:

> 'Cleveland Trust Company (CTC) is willing to decrease LHC's interest rate by one and a half points.' When our members grew upset and said, that's not even prime rate, Mr. Duncan said, 'I don't care. That's all you'll get from us. You can take it or leave it.' He added, 'Besides, nobody gets prime rate.' We only wish General Motors and the Eaton Corporation had heard that. No matter, because Mr. Duncan was right: That's all CTC would do![37]

Finally, Buckeye mentioned that Cleveland Trust had not mentioned its involvement with the Buckeye Neighborhood Housing Services. Buckeye explained it was because Cleveland Trust had not paid its dues to the NHS and had withdrawn its support.

In January 1980, the Federal Reserve demanded a list of actions be agreed to by the newly renamed Ameritrust as a condition of gaining merger approval. The Federal Reserve required the following:

- Make available to the public an Ameritrust loan policy.
- Make available the appraisal standards used by Ameritrust in conjunction with real estate loans.
- Design and implement a training program that satisfactorily trains

Ameritrust employees in the requirements of fair housing laws.

- Maintain a log in each office where applications are accepted to record information for every real estate and consumer loan inquiry about race, national origin, age, marital status, terms and conditions of loan request, and disposition of request.
- Assist applicants in obtaining credit counseling or provide it.
- Take steps to make the public aware of the availability of policies and services suggested in the letter.[38]

Ameritrust balked only at the record keeping provision, saying it would be expensive and unfair unless all the other institutions were required to do likewise but the bank was still required to do so for a year. When they finally agreed, the merger was approved.

Buckeye filed a protest against the decision and publicly called it a disappointment, claiming that the decision only answered some of the concerns.

Pat Kinney, a lead organizer on the issue, had expected the merger to be rejected however, Sharon Bryant called it a victory and said that a blocked merger would have been a disaster for BWCC and other groups who were following its lead in challenging banking practices.

Bryant believed that if the Federal Reserve had blocked the merger, the corporations of Cleveland would have declared war on the groups and would have destroyed them by ending their funding. The groups would have become a threat, instead of just a nuisance, and the corporate sector of Cleveland would have done to them what it had done to Kucinich.[39]

The Federal Reserve ruling did result in meaningful reforms that made it easier for community groups to document the bank's activities and to build cases for further challenges. It was the start of earning some accountability from the banks. The Federal Reserve also told Ameritrust to meet with BWCC and to end its stonewalling.

Buckeye's experience with its Cleveland Trust challenge set the stage for the first real negotiations between Ameritrust and BWCC and set an example for the community organizations of Cleveland. Soon Union Miles Community Coalition launched a similar challenge to Society National Bank, and Near West Neighbors in Action challenged Central National Bank.

Three factors contributed to this upsurge in action. One was the experience BWCC had developed in tackling the banks. BWCC shared that experience with other Cleveland groups. Second, the CRA and HMDA opened up windows of opportunity in dealing with redlining, that had never before been available to the groups. Finally, national networks, and organizations such as the National People's Action and the Center for Community Change were assembling the expertise and experience needed to help local groups become active on the issue.

Meanwhile, Buckeye found that, although it now could meet with Ameritrust, it was not going to be easy to reach an agreement with them. At the first meeting with M. Brock Weir, BWCC presented a half-dozen demands for various lines of credit and financing packages. The only point to which Ameritrust agreed was to advertise in the BWCC newsletter.

The war was not over between Ameritrust and Buckeye. The year 1980 was spent in fruitless meetings in which Ameritrust displayed its old intransigence beneath a veneer of cooperation. The new year presented another opportunity for BWCC to challenge Ameritrust when the bank applied to the Federal Reserve for permission to merge with some of its subsidiaries in outlying counties on February 23, 1981. On March 20, BWCC filed a challenge.

This time Buckeye was not alone in its challenge. It was joined by the Union Miles Community Coalition, Citizens to Bring Broadway Back, and the St. Clair Superior Coalition under the banner of Neighborhood People in Action (NPIA), a flag of convenience used by the groups for their larger campaigns.

NPIA's case was based on testimony and evidence presented by each group about its experiences with Ameritrust. It covered mortgage loan activities, Ameritrust's compliance with requirements from the 1980 challenge, the bank's continued lack of interest in working with neighborhood organizations, and poor commercial credit services. NPIA emphasized the contrast between Ameritrust and other banks that showed a more cooperative attitude toward the neighborhoods.

On December 1, 1981, the Federal Reserve approved the Ameritrust merger. The points raised against Ameritrust were written off by the review board as a reflection of market forces, legitimate management decisions, and individual corporate philosophy. The board did not cite any violations of its previous orders from 1980, and suggested that the mergers would not be to the detriment of the banking industry or the inconvenience of the public.

The second challenge took place in a changing world, both for the banks of Cleveland and the neighborhoods. The banks were entering a period of merger and consolidation that would witness the disappearance of many of the most famous banking names: Ameritrust, Society National Bank, and Central National Bank. It was also the time that saw the departure of that quintessential symbol of banking's old guard, M. Brock Weir. He retired as CEO in December 1983, moved to California, and left explicit instructions that his phone number not be given to anyone in Cleveland.

Weir's hostility to the neighborhoods may have backfired on him. BWCC's Kinney felt that Weir's belligerent style contributed to his departure from Ameritrust and the eventual demise, through merger, of the institution. Like a king obsessed with foreign wars while his kingdom decayed, Weir's conflicts distracted him from taking care of the bank's business during a time of upheaval and change in the banking industry. The rest of the Cleveland banking industry learned from the CRA fight between Ameritrust, BWCC and NPIA. Other banks took notice of Weir's situation to move in on Ameritrust's markets. They also realized that it would not take much to keep the neighborhood groups satisfied and was not worth a time-consuming, reputation-ruining, and expensive war with them in the name of corporate sovereignty.[40]

Challenges such as the one launched by BWCC and NPIA helped change the atmosphere in Cleveland about redlining. Financial institutions took notice and began to cooperate with local neighborhood groups. Often, that cooperation was encouraged by a CRA challenge, as was seen with Union Miles and Society National Bank, or Near West Neighbors in Action and Central National Bank.

The outcome was mixed. Banks began to appoint CRA officers who were vice-presidents and who seldom had the power to make anything happen beyond donations of office supplies and printing services for the neighborhood groups. Sometimes a real program was launched, as with Near West Housing Corporation, which put together a home purchase/rehab loan program in cooperation with Central National Bank using Urban Development Action Grant money from the city. Financial institutions also participated in development corporation boards that were spinoffs of the old groups, such as Bank on Buckeye, the Union Miles Development Corporation, and the Broadway Area Development Corporation. Even the old nemesis of the groups, Ameritrust, formed the Ameritrust Development Bank.

In the end one can ask whether the credit needs of Cleveland's neighborhoods are being met. This issue has been masked by the evolution of a community development infrastructure as represented by such organizations as the Cleveland Housing Network, the Enterprise Foundation, Neighborhood Progress Inc., and the Local Initiatives Support Corporation. There was a strong push to build new housing in Cleveland, which was given muscle with the success of Mayor Michael R. White in securing commitments from Cleveland's financial institutions to finance inner city housing development.

But the issue of the credit needs of Cleveland's neighborhoods has not been resolved. It manifests itself in new ways, and involves new institutions, such as the rise in the 1990s of predatory lending, and a plethora of check cashing, and payday loan companies, many of them owned by the same banking interests that the groups fought in the 1970s and 1980s. The surge in foreclosures also calls into question if real progress has been made.

Cleveland continues to have a two-tier financial services industry: one for the middle and upper classes, one for the poor. An issue from the past remains an issue for the present and future.

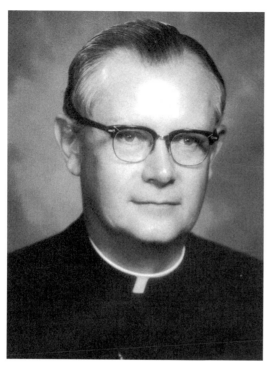

BISHOP JAMES A. HICKEY

Photo Credits:
Archives of the Diocese of Cleveland

AUXILIARY BISHOP WILLIAM COSGROVE

Rev. Dan Reidy

Harry Fagan

George Forbes and Dennis Kucinich in a rare moment of amity.

L to R: Norm Krumholz, unidentified man, Dennis Kucinich, Bob Weisman, Betty Grdina, unidentified man.

Dennis Kucinich congratulates George Voinovich on his victory Nov. 1979.

All Photo Credits This Page: Cleveland Press Archives, Cleveland State University

TOM GANNON

GLORIA ARON

*Neighborhood People in Action marching on SOHIO's
stockholders meeting April 1982.*

Chapter 7

Putting the Community into Community Development

They were young people and older people and if I were to see
them on the street I'd never think that this older woman would go
downtown, sit in at the office of the head of community development with a cardboard gun on a band around her head saying,
'You guys are holding a gun to our head and we're not going away
until you give us our money.'[1]

Gloria Aron, *Near West Neighbors in Action*

One of the most important sources of revenues for Cleveland in the 1970s and
1980s was the federal Community Development Block Grant (CDBG) program.
Control of millions of dollars coming into Cleveland under this program sparked
years of conflict. At the beginning, the CDBG money was perceived by the administration of Mayor Ralph Perk as a giant slush fund for a revenue-starved city. Within
the hierarchy of city council, the distribution of CDBG funds was a tool that council
leadership used to reward friends and punish enemies. At the bottom of the food
chain were the neighborhoods that were supposed to be beneficiaries of the program.

One of the most important campaigns of the community groups of Cleveland
was to claim the funds and wrestle control away from those who had dominated
CDBG decision making since the start of the program in 1974. The campaign to
reform the use of CDBG was fought on a citywide, neighborhood and block level.

The first major fight was over use of CDBG money to purchase the Cleveland

Arena in 1976, led by the Buckeye Woodland Community Congress (BWCC). BWCC was primed to lead the fight on this issue for several reasons. One was its own experience with ill-administered city programs and even more ill-administered federal programs, as was seen in the fight with the Department of Housing and Urban Development (HUD) over FHA practices. The neighborhood was also being denied its share of CDBG money for residents' home repairs.

In May 1976, Buckeye met with Ruth Miller, head of community development for the city of Cleveland. Miller told BWCC that no CDBG money was available for housing rehab in that area. This revelation was followed by an announcement in late June by Mayor Perk that the city planned to spend over $1 million dollars of CDBG money to purchase the land on which the old Cleveland Arena sat for a youth center. The purchase would bail out sports promoter Nick Mileti, for whom the arena was a money pit.

Joe Mariano of Buckeye described the resulting fireworks: "People were pissed. Suddenly the city had money to buy this arena. Folks went ballistic. 'What's going on here? How can the city tell us there's no money, then buy the arena?" [2]

A community meeting was called by Buckeye with a representative of the mayor, who spoke about the project. He was told to leave when he told BWCC what they didn't want to hear. BWCC sent a delegation to Congressman Louis B. Stokes' office to demand an investigation of the arena proposal. Then the Perk administration announced a public hearing on the proposal to turn the arena into a youth center. Groups opposing the project were told not to bother attending because they wouldn't change the city's plans. As Margaret Foster of Buckeye testified before the U.S. Congress,

> At a public meeting concerning use of community development funds to buy the arena, over 200 people voiced strong opposition to the city's plans. Other residents suggested that about $100 of community development money be used to purchase the mayor a hearing aid so that he and his city administration might hear what the citizens were saying. [3]

Ken Kovach, president of Buckeye, presented the neighborhood's case in a July 28, 1976 letter to David O. Meeker, an assistant secretary of HUD. Among the points he made were that citizen participation was discouraged when a public meeting was held, and they had been advised that opposition to the proposal was futile. Overall lack of support for the proposal was evident in public meetings at which virtually nobody spoke in favor of it.

Mayor Perk's administration pressured both local newspapers to support the proposal. Community Development Director Ruth Miller's husband, Forest City Enterprises CEO Sam Miller, was in business with the holder of the mortgage on the arena. Kovach petitioned Meeker to immediately begin an investigation of the proposal. [4]

The combination of neighborhood protests and complaints about city practices to HUD led to the collapse of political support for the project. The finance committee of city council refused to hold hearings on it. The final *coupe de grace* came when City Council President George Forbes announced his opposition to the project. The project was dead within two months of its proposal.

In the aftermath of the arena fight, a new actor joined the fray, the Cleveland Committee of the Citizens' Coalition for Block Grant Compliance (CCBGC). This coalition was formed in August 1976 by the League of Women Voters to monitor the use of CDBG funds. In Cleveland, members of the coalition included the League of Women Voters, the YWCA, the Cuyahoga Plan, the Commission on Catholic Community Action, and the Commission on Church and Society of the Greater Cleveland Interchurch Council.

The objective of the coalition was to see that municipalities followed the mandates of the 1974 Community Development Act establishing the CDBG program, namely to implement real citizen participation and to spend the money where it was supposed to be spent.

While individual neighborhood groups concentrated on the "what" of CDBG spending, the coalition concentrated on the "how," the process of citizen participation in deciding the content of CDBG applications.

The Cleveland Committee hit the Perk administration for its citizen participation process of "listenings," in which citizens were invited to comment on a CDBG application that had already been written and was on its way to HUD. Phil Star of CCBGC wondered aloud about the logic of the city's actions. "We wonder what their real intent is in involving citizens," he asked. "If they have already submitted it (the application) for review, why hold the hearings?"[5]

The Cleveland Committee began to build its case soon after its founding. The committee reviewed the city of Cleveland's Grant Performance Report for 1976-77, but it did not answer questions about funding for citizen participation, the number of people who had participated, who was involved in a city wide task force, the protocol of submitting proposals from agencies, and other points.[6]

The activities that should have been involved in citizen participation were contained in a Cleveland Committee report titled *Citizen Participation: Suggestions for Opening the Door for All Citizens.* This report stated:

> A review of the Grantee Performance Report established that there
> are three distinct points at which citizen participation is required.
> First, there must be citizen involvement in drawing up the citizen
> participation plan. Second, citizens must be given an opportunity
> to comment on proposals and make their own suggestions. Third,
> citizens should be involved in the development of criteria for evaluation and be involved in the evaluation in order to insure that citizen comments are taken into account. At the present time, it seems

that only the second level of participation is open to citizens and there has only been minimal participation in this phase.[7]

As one year's CDBG application was sent off to HUD, another year's application was being planned. If 1976 was a disappointment, 1977 did not promise much improvement. In a letter from Star to Ruth Miller dated May 11, 1977, Star reminds Miller of promises made and progress planned at an April 12th meeting on improving citizen participation. The committee had anticipated being contacted about public forums and being involved in making them a success, but the city had not contacted them since the April 12 meeting, and the committee learned by word of mouth about the first hearing, scheduled for May 17. Star wrote:

> We are concerned that, once again, like last year, only a few knowledgeable people will attend, that the program will be discussed in terms that few will grasp, and that most people will either not attend the hearings or, if they possibly see the ads, will not carry on a dialogue in their neighborhoods.[8]

Star concludes the letter with an offer and criticism:

> Our Committee stands ready to help prepare literature to be distributed to residents of Cleveland, to help distribute flyers and posters, and to try to involve people in the neighborhoods. But we cannot do this without some cooperation from you.[9]

No responses from the city to Star's letter could be found in the archives of the Catholic Diocese of Cleveland, which contain the files of the CCBGC. Whatever response there may have been was not enough to deter CCBGC from its next step.

On July 27 1977, the coalition got the city's attention. It filed an administrative complaint with the U.S. Department of Housing and Urban Development. Respondents in the complaint were Patricia Harris, secretary of HUD, Paul G. Lydens, director of the Columbus office of HUD, and Ralph J. Perk, mayor of Cleveland. The complainants were the Cleveland Committee of the Citizen's Coalition for Block Grant Compliance, the Community Development Committee of the Buckeye Woodland Community Congress, Housing Advocates, Inc., the Commission on Catholic Community Action, the League of Women Voters, and six east and west side Cleveland residents.

The complaint focused on a number of the program's failings in Cleveland: that CDBG funds were used for purposes forbidden by the 1974 Community Development Act, that money had been used to reduce, rather than increase community development activities, that it had failed to promote fair housing, and that the citizen participation process was inadequate. Throughout, the complaint focused on the inadequacy and poor quality of CDBG reporting and evaluation in Cleveland.

Two targets of the complaint were the Concentrated Crime Patrol (CCP) program of the Cleveland Police Department and the use of CDBG monies to reduce funding of city and non-profit agencies.

The Concentrated Crime Patrol program was promoted as a way to reduce crime by assigning more personnel to CDBG target areas. However, no additional police had been assigned to the areas. It was an example of the budgetary desperation of a financially strapped city. To maintain staffing and funding for the police, the administration annually raided the CDBG budget of $1,050,000.[10] Not only was the CCP a sham, it violated the provisions of the 1974 Community Development legislation that stated that CDBG moneys could not bail out financially strapped cities: it could only be used to improve services in target areas.

The city used a similar strategy with the Housing Division of the Department of Community Development. It used $500,000 of CDBG money to pay personnel and administrative expenses of the division and diverted an equal amount to pay the salaries of its inspectors under the guise of a concentrated code enforcement program. As with the police, the spending levels of the division did not increase; in fact, they decreased as a result of the retirement of two inspectors. CDBG moneys also were used to replace normal funding in the redevelopment, rehabilitation, and relocation and property management divisions of the department. All such activities, as in the case of the police, fell outside the permitted uses and mission of the CDBG program.

The final parts of the complaint dealt with fair housing and citizen participation. As to fair housing, the complaint documented past court cases that held the city guilty of intentional racial discrimination in housing policies. In the face of this history, the city did not include in its performance reports, documents required for its affirmative action programs to promote fair housing. It was joined in this violation by failure of the Columbus office of HUD to police the requirement.

In citizen participation, the city failed to document a citizen participation plan. The complaint states, "The city of Cleveland has no citizen participation plan beyond a general notion that it must conduct public hearings prior to submission of the CDBG application." [11]

Not only was the city unprepared to run the program: but it also was unprepared to respond to the complaint. In the closing days of the Perk administration, the level of confusion was revealed in the number of extensions the city was given by HUD to respond. In a letter to Ruth Miller from Stephen W. Brown, acting HUD director in Columbus, dated November 3, 1977, the city was warned that sanctions were imminent if it did not immediately submit its response to HUD.

Soon after that letter was received, time ran out on the Perk administration, and it was up to the Kucinich administration to build on the rubble of the past. Negotiations among HUD, the Kucinich administration, and the block grant coalition continued for almost a year until a settlement was reached early in July 1978.

The city promised to spend 80% of current and future funding to benefit low and moderate-income persons. It would continue to use funds to pay fifty police officers, but these officers would work exclusively in targeting areas under the guidance of the local communities. The coalition would withdraw its request to HUD to investigate the city and to order return of past CDBG funds. The fair housing complaint was not resolved.[12]

The complaint served notice on the city that the days were over when the true intent and purpose of the CDBG program could be sidestepped, subverted, and disregarded. The provisions of the program would have to be taken seriously. The coalition launched similar complaints in the suburbs of Cuyahoga County, and was not active on the issue in Cleveland after the July 1978 settlement with the city.

The Kucinich administration, in office only two years, did not have the opportunity to create much of a legacy in CDBG policy. It was preoccupied with the complaint that had been filed at the end of the Perk administration. It also had its own normal fights over individual items in the CDBG budget.

It defunded a number of development corporations in a bid to use CDBG dollars to repair sewers and faced localized battles in the St. Clair Superior and Near West Side neighborhoods that were as much about local politics as CDBG policies. Kucinich's CDBG requests were routinely held hostage in the war between the administration and City Council President George Forbes.

The chaos was even noted in an unfavorable review that HUD gave the administration in February 1979. In spring 1979, $37 million was held up in a game of chicken between Kucinich and Forbes, which was finally resolved in the last moment. Kucinich's administration did a better job of implementing citizen participation, until such events as the uproar at the neighborhoods conference made them shy about public forums that could turn against them.

It was under the Voinovich administration that CDBG policy, as it exists today in Cleveland, took shape. Director of Community Development Vince Lombardi found that the city faced a very unfavorable review by HUD auditors. The audit reported numerous violations of regulations, and the auditors noted that they had not been able to find responsible officials to talk to for their review. According to Star, the Voinovich administration listened to citizen input, and did not try to dodge the regulations. By 1981, the city had received more favorable audits for March and September of the year.[14]

The two most important features of the Voinovich approach were that CDBG funding was integrated into a long-term strategic plan for the city and that a historic compromise was reached with city council on CDBG funding. This compromise was the result of a fight with council early in the new administration. Forbes made sure the new administration knew who was boss in early tiffs over details of CDBG proposals that were reminiscent of his dealings with Kucinich. Under the compromise, half of the CDBG funds were spent according to the administration's priorities; the other half on the council's priorities, which meant that individual city council members could expect to receive a certain amount of CDBG money. The details of who got what depended on the pecking order within city council. With this arrangement, the formerly wild and woolly world of council politics regarding community development money settled down into an established system.

Although the Voinovich administration began to put its CDBG house in order, problems persisted. Bad reviews from HUD on the city's performance continued. The reports gave credit for improvement but the threat of funding cutoffs and sanctions made it appear as if the normal state of the program was one of chronic crisis. There was always more thunder than lightning in HUD's admonitions, however. Money kept flowing.

Star did not blame any particular administration for this semi-permanent state of crisis. The problem was a city that had been rated at one time as one of the best-managed in the nation, had become a basket case by the 1970s. The competent people, who could leave, had left. Able talent that had come to Cleveland to serve in the Stokes administration and had stayed on felt overwhelmed. With such a legacy of neglect and decay, it would have been miraculous had any program been well run in Cleveland, much less one so complex and lucrative as the CDBG program.[15]

Issues of block grant spending became local after the 1978 settlement of the HUD complaint. The conflicts that did arise revolved around some basic issues: how community development money was unevenly distributed; how CDBG money was considered the private property of city council and how decisions were made behind closed doors; and how CDBG money was frequently wasted in projects neighborhoods did not want or by paying incompetent contractors.[16]

One complicating issue on the Near West Side was the issue of turf claimed by adjoining neighborhood groups. The area west of West 65 Street had activists and block clubs who felt more at home with Near West Neighbors In Action (NWNIA), although Detroit Superior Community Development Organization (DSCDO) argued that it was their turf. This pro-NWNIA sentiment came from such leaders as Gloria Aron on West 81 Street who had a long organizing history with the West Side Community House where NWNIA was originally housed.

Residents of West 81 Street wanted new sidewalks. Councilwoman Mary Zone refused to help, and sent them to DSCDO for help, where they learned that in order to get help with sidewalks, they would have to participate in a code enforcement program, which would survey their street for housing code violations and, as some had indelicately put it, turn in their neighbors. They were told this was a requirement of the the Cleveland Department of Community Development. Residents were not interested in doing the work of the housing inspectors, and they did not want to set neighbor against neighbor.

Bob Pollack, an organizer for Near West Neighbors in Action, and future head of Near West Housing Corporation described the implications:

> We didn't want to be the ones the city could point the finger at and

say we are doing this because Lenny Strimple (a NWNIA activist) and these folks over here voted to have it done. And then Lenny Strimple is going to have his house firebombed or get shot at by his neighbor who is running a business out of his back yard repairing cars...or just got cited for $3,000 to $5,000 worth of repair work.

Another problem facing the program, according to Pollack, was the economics of inner city housing.

Those properties had very little equity in them because the appraised values were so low. They would start code enforcement and the absentee owner was hard to go after, so the person you could get the victory on was the little old lady who was on a Social Security income. Once they started inspecting the property, they had that policy that if you are going to get any money from the city, you had to bring the whole house up to code. Often that worked out to more than the house was worth. Then you are going down the road to condemn the property and maybe throw this woman out on the street. [17]

Near West engaged the issue with the usual arsenal of weapons available to the groups: public meetings with a hapless bureaucrat as the main meal and street theater in the corridors of city hall. In one community meeting the mayor was treated to a skit using themes lifted from The Godfather. Gloria Aron described the skit:

First we did the skit, and one of the neighbors on my street was dressed up as a gangster... You know, striped suit, black tie, and black shirt, and he had a violin case with 'city hall' written on it or 'department of community development.' I was dressed up as a little old lady, and basically; it was him knocking on the door. This was about the VIP and the CASH program, which some people in our neighborhood were having real problems with, and the guy from the city said, 'I have a deal that you can't refuse.' [18]

Aron described another encounter with Vince Lombardi, director of community development for Mayor Voinovich:

We held a meeting and asked Vince Lombardi to come out. We had put down things we want. Well, the very first thing we wanted to know was if he would give us our sidewalks, and as soon as he said, 'No,' we said, 'Get out.' He said, 'But wait, I want to talk.' We said, 'If your answer to the question is no, then there is nothing to talk about.' [19]

In another action at city hall, activists from Near West Neighbors in Action wore headbands with cutout pistols attached to say that city hall was holding a gun to their heads. Bob Pollack described the meeting:

> I was just doing everything I could to keep from cracking up because of everybody standing there with the headbands. They're like the killer bees from *Saturday Night Live*. I think it was so disarming to Lombardi because these people are sitting there quoting Community Development Block Grant regs and he was looking at this assemblage of people thinking, 'What the hell is going on here?' [20]

Near West finally got a meeting with Mayor Voinovich on the issue. The mayor asked Lombardi if any regulations in the CDBG program required the code enforcement program. Lombardi said no, and the program died there.

The West 81st Street block club allied with NWNIA until NWNIA expanded its boundaries to include them. It worked with NWNIA, St.Clair Superior Coalition, and Union Miles Community Coalition, who were having the same problems. The West 81st Street block club got its sidewalks. As Aron said, "I'm not sure now, looking back on it, that that was the best use of community development funds, but at that time, that was what the money was being used for." [21]

Two accomplishments of the CDBG organizing during this time in Cleveland were lasting: It helped educate a generation of neighborhood staff people and leaders in the mundane, technical, and critical details of such programs as CDBG, and expertise was developed and shared throughout the neighborhoods. It also laid the foundations for future neighborhood development work.

In the Broadway area, CDBG organizing inspired the creation of Barkwell Park on the site of a former elementary school. The local neighborhood had tried to save the old school for a community center. The building was too dilapidated, and had to be demolished. Next, the community decided on the idea of creating a park on the vacant lot. Community development money was secured and neighborhood residents took over the planning process to design a park that is still one of the most enduring monuments to the organizing of the time. The victory was not only the creation of the park, but proof that the citizens could plan for their own community.

The second accomplishment is that CDBG organizing opened up funding for neighborhood-based organizations to begin housing development work. The origins of this policy actually had little to do with housing rehab at first. It started with the demolition, not the rehabilitation of vacant houses. By the third or fourth year of the CDBG program, the city had torn down almost 3,000 houses annually. At first, many neighborhood residents and organizations were relieved. The problem was that after the bulldozer was done, the neighborhood was left with a vacant lot. Some neighborhoods witnessed so much demolition that they resembled rural areas. In the Near West Side, a program called Project Secure boarded up open, vacant, and vandalized properties. The problem then was that when the houses were secured, they could no longer be demolished. So they sat, and the neighborhood had a new problem.

About this time, the Famicos Foundation was drawing attention to its lease purchase rehab program. Famicos's charismatic leader Bob Wolf drove home the message of rehab yes, demolition no. Neighborhood groups began to pay attention, and in 1981, the Cleveland Housing Network was born, and put housing rehab as the centerpiece of neighborhood development efforts.

How much "community" is there in community development? Federal regulations have been followed since the days of the Kucinich administration. Administrations are experienced enough to use the CDBG program to plan for the future of the funds. City council has its piece of the pie. The city is not as financially battered and close to the edge of the abyss as it was when the CDBG funds were looked upon as a last-chance slush fund. City council is more professional, educated, and financially secure than it was at the start of the CDBG program in 1974. Citizen participation now resides with the community development corporations that, to a large degree, owe their existence to the program.

It is not a question of how democratic the process of deciding on community development funds is; rather, it is a question of how democratic the non-profit sector is. This varies widely across the city. What it reflects is the degree to which community groups have been able to build the democratic capacities of the people in their communities.

In campaigns around the CDBG program, the city saw the development of many ordinary citizens who could plan Barkwell Park or who could go toe-to-toe with city hall bureaucrats on details of the program. With the professionalization of the neighborhood sector and the decline of organizing, talent at the grassroots level proved fleeting.

How much community is there in community development? The answer to that question always depends on the health and strength of the organized communities of Cleveland.

Chapter 8

"GIVE US A BILLION DOLLARS!"

It was symbolic of class war in a democratic society. [1]

Harry Fagan, *Commission on Catholic Community Action*

The energy crisis was a hallmark issue of the 1970s and 1980s. The Mideast oil embargo, skyrocketing prices at the fuel pump, and a series of severely cold winters combined with economic recession, propelled the issue onto the national agenda. Public debates raged over the energy future of society. Debate over nuclear power was fueled by the nuclear accident at Three Mile Island in Pennsylvania and movies such as *The China Syndrome*. For the first time in our nation's history, energy conservation and the search for alternative energy sources were taken seriously. This panoply of issues resonated in Cleveland's neighborhoods, whose residents were being whipsawed by the forces of economic recession and skyrocketing energy costs.

The First Target: East Ohio Gas

The first campaign on energy policies launched in Cleveland was directed at the East Ohio Gas Company. Shortages in natural gas hit the nation during one of the coldest winters on record, the winter of 1976-1977. Across the country, but especially in the northeast and midwest, utilities curtailed service to their industrial and commercial customers, resulting in plant closings that laid off more than a million workers in Ohio alone. In Ohio, a state of emergency was declared.

Debates on energy policy focused on the supply of natural gas and what it would take to deliver gas to consumers. The American Gas Association claimed supplies of natural gas were adequate, but because of government price controls, it did not pay producers to take the gas out of the ground. Its solution was to decontrol the price of natural gas. The advocates of decontrol theorized that a return to natural market prices would moderate prices and would attain a reasonable level with new suppliers entering the market, producing amounts of gas that were denied the public by regulation produced shortages. Critics responded that the natural market in an industry dominated by a handful of producers, pipelines, and utilities with a legal monopoly in their service areas was a free market fantasy.

The old energy regime was dead, and the winter of 1976-1977 was its funeral. The gas industry held most of the cards. In February 1977, in one of his first legislative victories, President Jimmy Carter secured passage of the Emergency Natural Gas Act. The act mandated government oversight to guarantee delivery of natural gas to critical industries and institutions. It also suspended the cap on gas prices until July 31, 1977. For a few months, the natural gas industry could have the deregulated market it wanted.

A more long-term victory for the natural gas industry was the passage of the Natural Gas Policy Act of 1978. The act defined the policy world that the community organizations would dwell in. It set up a system for the decontrol of natural gas keyed to the type of gas being pumped. Gas drilled before 1977 would remain regulated as before. New gas from wells drilled above 15,000 feet was to be gradually decontrolled until it reached parity with the price of oil in 1985. New, deep well gas drilled below 15,000 feet would be decontrolled altogether. The resulting price spike lit the fuse on the energy issue at the grassroots level as the nation was asked to adjust to a new, more expensive energy regime.

While the shape of this new price regime concerned community organizations in Cleveland, their immediate demands were more basic than the mix of new and old gas coming into the homes and businesses of the neighborhoods. The groups agitated for a number of reforms for how East Ohio did business. They wanted a no-shut-off policy during winter, senior citizen discounts, an end to estimated bills, and funding for home weatherization programs.

East Ohio officials promised to attend meetings, but did not show up. When David Sweet, chief of the Public Utilities Commission of Ohio, urged the gas company to help fund home weatherization programs, Dudley Taw, East Ohio's CEO, responded that the utility was not in the home repair business.

In 1979, protests began against East Ohio's request for a six point nine percent rate hike that reflected the spike in utility rates following the Natural Gas Policy Act. It also passed on to consumers a seventeen percent rate increase to reflect increased gas charges from its suppliers. The Senior Citizens Coalition (SCC) demanded that East Ohio's executives' salaries be trimmed to $50,000 per year, that the rate hike be withdrawn, and the EOG fund a lobbyist in Columbus for the coalition, as consumers had paid East Ohio lobbyists to raise their bills.

The Senior Citizens Coalition hit East Ohio on October 12, 1979 after meeting with EOG's public relations person at St. John College at the Catholic Diocese's complex down the street from East Ohio's corporate offices. At the meeting, the coalition's demands for a twenty five per cent discount for the elderly were rebuffed. Representatives of the coalition asked to speak with Dudley Taw. He was out of town. They tried to get into the utility's headquarters and were met by security guards and company employees, who blocked its doors. [2]

The utility wanted the groups to meet with David Talbot, head of public relations for the company. They wanted Taw. The group's frustration resulted in a hit on a Rocky River Presbyterian church, of which Dudley Taw was a member. The event included Agnes Jackson of Buckeye Woodland Community Congress (BWCC), lecturing a Sunday school class on justice for the neighborhoods. The demonstrators excommunicated Dudley Taw for the sin of freezing poor people with high gas bills. The Presbytery of Cleveland was not amused, and it shared its displeasure with the Cleveland Catholic Diocese and the Catholic Commission, leading to damage control by Harry Fagan. Sandra Kluk, executive director of BWCC, described the blowback.

> The reason it blew up in our face was that it was a church. There
> are just some things that are sacred to everybody. You can go to his
> home. That's ok. You can go to his place of business. That's ok. But
> his church, that's something else. There was a lot of backlash that I
> think even the commission had to deal with because of that. [3]

East Ohio Gas had no experience in dealing with groups laying siege to them. Dudley Taw hired Pat Carney for the public relations department of East Ohio to deal with the controversy. Carney had just come back to northeast Ohio after serving as a lobbyist in Washington. His first mission was to find out what East Ohio was dealing with.

Carney began to attend meetings, and said that if he went to work in the morning and did not see a picket line outside of East Ohio Gas's headquarters, he thought something must be wrong. He met with Fagan and discovered Saul Alinsky. Carney concluded that East Ohio was the target of a multi-issue movement, a social revolution with roots in socialism and liberation theology.[4]

The Senior Citizens Coalition continued to pursue Taw in vain. It met with East Ohio officials between hits. In January 1980, they attempted to pay gas bills with pennies at the downtown offices of National City Bank. Taw was on its board of trustees. The coalition demanded a twenty five per cent discount be given to the elderly, estimated bills be eliminated, monthly meter readings, not estimates, a rate freeze for two years, and only one fuel cost adjustment be made per year.

In these demands, there seemed to be some movement in the issues of the Senior Citizens Coalition. No mention is made of the home insulation program. The twenty-five percent senior discount rates, and an end to estimated bills and monthly meter readings were the same as previous demands from such groups as Buckeye Woodland Community Congress (BWCC), St.Clair Superior Coalition

(SCSC) and Citizens to Bring Broadway Back (CBBB). The rate demands reflected the revolving door rate hikes East Ohio had received in the past year, causing a forty percent rise in bills in one year. East Ohio continued to blame the rate increases on increasing prices from its suppliers.

The campaign against East Ohio was not simply a citywide campaign. Each neighborhood had its own campaign. Mark McDermott of CBBB said the group did not know how these issues would play out in the neighborhood. In the past, the group had worked on issues that offered easily achievable victories, such as a stoplight on Fenn Avenue, a new fire station, or dilapidated houses being torn down. CBBB did not know whether the East Ohio issue was centered enough on the self-interest of community residents to work. It worked well enough to produce meetings with hundreds of people in attendance.

A major complaint was excessive estimated meter readings. Some customers had not had their gas meters read in years. The volume of complaints to the Office of Consumer Counsel in Columbus reached a point that an investigation was launched. The East Ohio response was that it was hard to get into some residences to read the meter, and that estimates frequently underreported usage.[5] One solution, which is now standard, was to install outside meters.

Pat Carney helped to develop a consumer board to improve East Ohio's reputation and to open communications with its critics. Dudley Taw had been willing to work with Carney. Although he was from the traditional school of corporate management, he was also the one being beaten up. Taw's help was instrumental in bringing along the doubters on the utility's board. These moves accelerated under the leadership of the utility's new CEO, Dick Kelso, whom Carney credited for not only making peace with the community groups, but also building the best relations the utility had ever had with its unions.

East Ohio's rate request in the spring of 1980 brought a storm of protest. Cleveland city council held a hearing at which the Public Utilities Commission of Ohio (PUCO) and the Office of Consumer Counsel took testimony before 150 representatives of SCSC, BWCC, Union Miles Community Coalition (UMCC), the SCC, and CBBB. The April 29 hearing revealed not only the usual level of frustration with East Ohio, but also PUCO's lack of credibility after it repeatedly approved rate increases requested by East Ohio.

In August 1981, East Ohio won another rate hike of $43 million of a $59.2 million request. The response to the increase this time came from elected officials, such as Mayor Voinovich, and State Representative Benny Bonnano, who had launched an effort to get the PUCO commissioners elected. At the same time, EOG applied for another five point three percent rate increase. Of four rate increases granted since 1970, two were in 1980 and 1981.

Behind East Ohio's policies were a set of assumptions about the future of the gas market. EOG predicted one major spike in gas prices in the aftermath of the Natural Gas Policy Act, after which the market, freed from regulatory burdens, would not experience dramatic price rises as in the past. Other companies, such as Columbia Gas, read things differently and tied themselves into ruinous long-term contracts with suppliers.

East Ohio finally proposed a new formula for pricing to PUCO. It took the price of gas out of its profit calculations and proposed a one-for-one arrangement, in which if the prices of their suppliers went down one cent, rates for consumers also would go down one cent. The same applied to price increases. The utility no longer wanted to be in a commodities market as it had in the past, betting on the future price of natural gas from the well. The deal was made, and it guaranteed East Ohio a generation of peace on the consumer and community fronts.

Except for actions by the Senior Citizen Coalition in June 1982 over a proposed $70 million rate hike, organizing against East Ohio wore itself out. EOG finally convinced community groups that it was not to blame for the increase in gas prices, but was passing along price increases by its suppliers and pipelines. This claim was verified by a fact sheet prepared by National People's Action (NPA) showing the shift of the composition of the typical heating dollar from 1970 to 1980. In 1970, twenty six cents of every dollar went to the producer, twenty nine cents went to the pipeline, and forty five cents went to the utility. By 1980, the world had changed: fifty four cents went to the producer, twenty five cents went to the pipeline, and only twenty one cents went to the utility. The groups were starting to recognize that not all energy companies were the same.

Bill Callahan of Citizen Action described the split in corporate ranks:

> In a sense, it was not an anti-utility campaign. Columbia Gas had a big stake in the drilling and transportation industry, so they liked deregulation. East Ohio didn't like deregulation because it's just a distribution company. The gas distribution industry was really divided on the issue, and it was not for them that it was happening.[6]

The East Ohio campaign resulted in tangible accomplishments. East Ohio ceased winter shutoffs and under pressure from PUCO, finally cooperated with the demand to support home insulation programs.

An energy audit program, funded by East Ohio was begun. This generated applicants for a wide range of home insulation programs that proliferated through the early 1980s. As with many victories of organizing, these programs became a stable funding generator for the non-profit development groups.

The SOHIO Campaign

The campaign against East Ohio's rate hikes led to one of the most famous and disastrous campaigns of Cleveland's community organizations, the campaign against natural gas deregulation targeted at Standard Oil of Ohio (SOHIO).

The switch in focus to SOHIO began in early 1981. Taking the lead was

Neighborhood People in Action (NPIA). Organizations working on the issue were: Near West Neighbors in Action (NWNIA), BWCC, SCC, SCSC, UMCC, and CBBB.

The first goal of the campaign was to garner as much support as possible from local, state, and national politicians and representatives to fight the Reagan administration's plan to deregulate natural gas prices. The second goal was to secure from SOHIO, $1 billion to finance energy conservation and subsidy programs for low and moderate-income utility customers.

There were several reasons for the $1 billion demand from SOHIO. SOHIO was a local corporation whose staff played a prominent role in civic affairs. This gave the strategy a local handle to match the national focus of defeating natural gas decontrol. SOHIO was awash in cash to the point that it paid cash for its new headquarters on Cleveland's public square. It held enormous natural gas reserves that would become even more valuable if natural gas prices were deregulated.

Hubris was no small factor, behind the groups' willingness to take on as formidable a target as SOHIO. The groups were on a roll. They had national reach with their alliance with National People's Action. They routinely humbled recalcitrant bureaucrats. They had full time organizing staffs, held conventions that were attended by hundreds of members, and organized dozens of block clubs. They began to believe their own propaganda that they were giant killers.

The Ohio lobbying effort against natural gas deregulation was coordinated through a statewide coalition, the Ohio Action Coalition (OAC). The main goal of OAC was to get as much support as it could in Ohio's congressional delegation to combat natural gas deregulation. It arranged support for alternative legislation and lobbied intensively to have congressional hearings in Ohio take testimony on the impact of rising energy costs. The NPIA in Cleveland and the OAC statewide did not even talk to city councilmen without asking that they pass the word to their congressional representatives that natural gas deregulation should be defeated and that a congressional hearing be held in Ohio.

On the national level, one of the most prominent groups was the Citizen Labor Energy Coalition (CLEC), a group led by Citizen Action and the labor movement. OAC and NPA worked with CLEC, but there was no love lost between them. NPA and Citizen Action had little use for each other. The clash was based on differences in overall organizing philosophies, and how the two groups related to politicians.

CLEC was a coalition. It was compatible with the strategies of groups such as Citizen Action, which was oriented toward building coalitions with major national players, such as unions and senior citizens organizations, using high-quality research to affect local, state, or national political events and legislation. It had professional staff persons. It was not oriented toward organizing the unorganized or developing local leadership. Its focus was to organize already-existing leadership and organizations in communities.

NPA, although itself a coalition, was not involved with coalitions outside itself.

It was based on creating leadership and organizations in the communities in which it worked. Its style was to send out large numbers of organizers into communities using a rote manual of organizing. The goal was to produce numbers of block clubs and bodies to conventions, conferences, and actions. Issues were to come from the block clubs. It was a disciplined, if rigid, organization and took a shotgun approach to its organizing that often produced real leaders who could stand the test of time. [7]

Shel Trapp described what led to the break between NPA and CLEC. The American Petroleum Institute was holding its convention in Chicago in November 1981. This was the occasion for a series of actions and demonstrations billed as the "Shoot Out With Pig Oil." NPA was on its way to a hit. They were greeted by the Chicago Police Department, in force. CLEC had obtained a parade permit for the hit. Trapp went ballistic. The permit had violated a cardinal rule of NPA: Never tell the cops what you are doing. Trapp never forgave CLEC for the blunder and never worked with them again. [8]

The incident was not all there was behind the split between CLEC and NPA; there were strategic differences between them, as well. CLEC felt that the energy corporations were politically vulnerable. Their goal was to target potential swing districts represented by Republican congressmen who had come in on Reagan's coattails. CLEC launched a major effort to organize opposition to natural gas deregulation in these districts. The effort would concentrate on labor unions and senior citizens organizations.

A perfect example of CLEC's strategy could be seen in its work in the Toledo area, where it used canvassing by Citizen Action to proselytize against deregulation and to build a network of people whom it could use for future efforts. Bill Callahan, who worked on the issue for Citizen Action, defined the strategy as political terrorism against the proponents of deregulation. In the Toledo campaign, it was successful in unseating Ed Weber, a Republican elected with Reagan in a traditionally Democratic district, and replacing him with Democrat Marcie Kaptur. [9]

Meanwhile, NPA was working on the issue as it would any other with direct-action confrontation, where it would demand that the oil companies back off their campaign for deregulating natural gas. Callahan considered it a loser from the start. The group was confronting an industry around an issue considered a top priority by the industry, and would move heaven and earth to win. NPA groups could harass SOHIO's CEO Alton Whitehouse all they wanted, but Whitehouse was not going to go against a national policy proposal that would earn his company billions of dollars in profits. He would ignore them if he could. When he could not ignore the groups anymore, he would make phone calls to their funders. Either way, they would lose. [10]

In May 1981 NPIA launched the offensive against SOHIO by staging a sit-in in the lobby of the Midland Building, then its headquarters in downtown Cleveland. Pitt Curtiss, head of public relations for SOHIO, was called to the lobby by security. Curtiss described the scene:

I went down to the lobby to try and interface with the group to find out what was causing this. The issue of natural gas deregulation was hard to determine for a while because the group was insisting that they wanted to talk to SOHIO's chairman, who wasn't available. I finally got the group to leave after a good deal of discussion by agreeing to make Al Whitehouse aware of the group's presence. [11]

At the end of September, the group started to pin down details of a meeting with Pitt Curtiss. It decided on a smaller meeting for October 7, 1981. Preparations included both a leadership meeting and an energy issue staff meeting to prepare leaders for the upcoming meeting with SOHIO.

At these early stages of the campaign, questions about the SOHIO effort, foretold future problems. There was considerable skepticism about whether the billion-dollar goal was realistic. The groups constantly wondered about where SOHIO was coming from and what its strategy would be. Staff meeting notes reflected doubts about the preparedness of leaders for negotiations. They were worried that there had not been enough role playing or thinking through different scenarios in a preparatory game called 'What if?' in which all sorts of possible developments were thought out ahead of time. They were also concerned that there was not enough explanation of the origins of the issue. Finally, doubts about the reliability of information abounded, expressed in notes from staff meetings.

Sandra Kluk, lead organizer for the SOHIO campaign for BWCC, described the concerns of organizers:

> It was part hesitation and part wanting to make sure we were covering ourselves because we were taking on a much bigger target. We were also very careful about this stuff, and we really wanted to make sure we had community support. We knew it was going to be a major event. We were also concerned that if we did get a meeting with Alton Whitehouse and SOHIO, were our leaders ready for it? Were they trained to the point where they could come up against someone like an Alton Whitehouse?[12]

The groups settled on three basic demands going into the October meeting: the billion-dollar demand to fund weatherization and energy assistance, assurance that SOHIO would oppose the deregulation of natural gas, and confirmation that a meeting would be arranged with Alton Whitehouse.

Pitt Curtiss, the public relations head for SOHIO, provided the best description of the October 7 meeting:

> The way the evening developed, I was seated as an audience of one confronted with a series of skits depicting the difficulties con-

fronting low-income people as a result of the threat of natural gas deregulation. I suspect those skits went on for about thirty minutes, and I sat there as a polite and interested audience.

Curtiss responded that natural gas was not a big profit center for SOHIO, a minor supplier in the United States, in spite of the enormous gas reserves held in Alaska. His message was not well received:

> I was continually interrupted during this discussion, and wasn't certain that I was really able to make the point I wanted to make. I suspect that there was a total disbelief about SOHIO's position in this because the demand was being made that we contribute a billion dollars. [13]

Based on notes from the October 12 staff meeting reviewing the October 7 meeting, there was little to celebrate. From the meeting notes, the staff was impressed with Pitt Curtiss and embarrassed that he was better prepared than they were. Curtiss was also good at manipulating their leaders and at diverting attention from SOHIO and onto the city. Anger and impatience were expressed regarding the lack of good intelligence about SOHIO.

In contrast to the meeting notes in the BWCC archives, Sandra Kluk recalled that Curtiss was so successful at alienating people that BWCC considered him a godsend:

> Every time that man opened his mouth, somebody came to our side, including the media. The media was actually a friend at that point on the issue we were doing and also were angry at SOHIO. Curtiss was being very abrasive, speaking down to people, and they really reacted to that. He was actually good for us. [14]

More significant than tactical worries were concerns over the entire campaign. Comments from the October 12 meeting reveal a level of discomfort: "Do folks still buy the idea of Standard Oil giving money?" and "Having no other demand is hurting us."

While NPIA was trying to figure out SOHIO, SOHIO was trying to figure out NPIA. SOHIO sent a delegation to Carney at East Ohio for advice on handling the groups. Carney responded that it was not going to be easy.

The next staff meeting on October 23 discussed moving on to an actual meeting with Alton Whitehouse. Attendees reviewed the earlier meeting with Curtiss, the outcome of a public meeting, and an educational program on the results of the decontrol of natural gas prices. Several points were resolved: They did not want to meet with Curtiss; they wanted Alton Whitehouse. They resolved to do better in future meetings: "Lets not embarrass ourselves again."

SOHIO had put an offer on the table: Whitehouse would meet with three representatives at the Standard Oil building. NPIA staff response was mixed: "Meet with him." "Meet with him with fifteen leaders." "Fuck him and hit him." No resolution was recorded in the meeting.

The meeting ended with a push for intensive research about Whitehouse, what clubs he belonged to, what properties he owned, and any upcoming events where he might be speaking.

The energy staff meeting of November 18 was a preparation for a public meeting that would be held at UMCC. The public meeting would educate leadership and the rank and file about the issues of the campaign, the history of negotiations, the history of SOHIO, and the thinking behind the demands. The meeting would also decide how to respond to the offer from SOHIO. The options were laid out: a) "Accept small meeting with SOHIO on our own terms;" b) "If screwed in small meeting, we hit him;" and c) "Other?" A possible visit to this meeting by NPA leader Gail Cincotta was mentioned.

The meeting with Whitehouse and Curtiss was held on December 8. The demands of the delegation from NPIA were that SOHIO oppose the deregulation of natural gas, that SOHIO provide $1 billion dollars for energy assistance in the state of Ohio, and that Whitehouse attend local neighborhood energy hearings. No reports on the result of the meeting, other than that provided Curtiss, could be located. Curtiss remembered:

> The meeting lasted for perhaps a half an hour when we became aware that NPIA had issued a news release to the local media saying they were confronting SOHIO about a billion-dollar contribution. That just finished it right there. We had at that point said, 'This isn't what we had in mind." Whitehouse was very upset. He left the meeting, and I don't blame him. I sat with the group. In a very nice way, I said to them, 'You screwed this up. You turned us off.' [15]

Both sides backed off for the holiday season and took stock of the situation as they entered 1982, a year that was to be one of the most important in the life of the community organizing movement in Cleveland.

Chasing Whitehouse around northeast Ohio was not the only activity of the campaign. Preparations were made for pushes in winter and spring to gain the support of other groups and institutions in the fight against deregulation. The winter and early spring of 1982 were taken up by organizing a congressional hearing in Cleveland and a forum at Cleveland State University on natural gas deregulation.

A major focus of this effort was the religious community of Cleveland. Bishop Anthony Pilla of the Cleveland Catholic Diocese was approached to have the diocese oppose deregulation, to have the state conference of bishops do the same, and to approve workshops on the issue to be held in area churches. The Cleveland State event was successful, drawing an audience of over 500 people. The congressional hearing ensured that Citizen Action, the Citizen Labor Energy Coalition, and NPIA never worked together again locally.

Attending the hearing were NPIA, Citizen Action, the United Auto Workers (UAW), and U.S. Senator Howard Metzenbaum. Citizen Action and the UAW were in a love fest with Metzenbaum. NPIA was looking for a confrontation and a demand to make on Metzenbaum who was already a stalwart against deregulation. They hit a natural ally. The behavior of NPIA at this forum resulted in a series of letters to NPIA protesting the treatment of Senator Metzenbaum. Citizen Action and the UAW were interested in building a coalition. NPIA considered itself to be the leader on the issue. To Bill Callahan, it was a fundamental strategic weakness of the NPIA approach that he found appalling:

> That is the most fundamental breakdown in organizing you could possibly have. You are in a room with leadership and they are not trying to figure out who they are, how they operate, and what their self interest is. From the earliest Alinsky definition of how you do this stuff, there is nothing more important than understanding the other party's self interest. You walk into a room and say this is the way it ought to be. You've got to deal with us. You're defining people as a target and you haven't done an analysis of them. That level of sophistication was a big problem. [16]

The focus of the spring activities for NPIA was the upcoming demonstration at the April 22 1982 stockholders meeting of SOHIO to be held at the palatial Stouffer's Hotel, (now the Renaissance Hotel) on Cleveland's public square. There was a two-part action plan. First, the NPIA group had collected about 100 proxy votes from sympathetic institutions and individuals, so that their representatives could be present at the stockholders meeting. The second part was a demonstration and picket line outside of the hotel to protest the corporate policies of SOHIO and to gain public attention for NPIA's energy campaign.

SOHIO had anticipated this move in the aftermath of the Chicago Shoot Out With Pig Oil demonstrations in November 1981. It began to monitor stock transactions to see whether any group was purchasing blocks of stock that could be used for proxies to gain entrance to the stockholders meeting. As Curtiss recalled:

> The thought occurred to us, [that] a disruption of the annual meeting would not be out of order for this group. So we followed the purchase of stock, saw where a member of (NPA leader) Gail Cincotta's staff [had] purchased a block of stock. That was a clear signal. [17]

The plans NPIA had made for its activities that day did not hold up under the excitement and pressure of the moment. Security was all over the hotel but, by some fluke, the front entrance of Stouffer's had been left unguarded. Demonstrators outside the hotel, numbering in the hundreds, entered the hotel lobby. Neighborhood people blowing penny whistles, and waving banners and placards occupied the lobby, and filled the ornate stairway that led to the stockholders' meeting.

At the meeting, SOHIO management refused to recognize speakers representing NPIA. The NPIA contingent advanced on the stage where the officials were seated and a confrontation ensued. Officers of the board abruptly declared the meeting adjourned. The shortest, most tumultuous stockholders meeting in SOHIO history was over.

Organizers of the demonstration thought that they had shut down the meeting themselves, however, Curtiss maintained that the abrupt ending had been a conscious decision made by the company beforehand. He said:

> We had expected that the meeting would be disrupted. We
> planned to deal with it: Call the meeting to order, announce the
> vote of proxies, and adjourn the meeting.[18]

Curtiss and SOHIO hit back at the groups in a media campaign that challenged the legitimacy of the protest. Curtiss recalled:

> In the aftermath of that meeting, we met further with the media to
> make sure to reinforce what the original issue seemed to be, but
> what was now taking place was a result of the Chicago influence.
> It was masterminded by the Chicago people. They were the ones
> who came up to the registration desk and tried to run things their
> way. We had cameras there. We were getting pictures of every-
> body, so we knew who was whom. [19]

SOHIO was conscious of the media attention, felt on the defensive, and responded accordingly. The company viewed the media as a liberal institution that would naturally favor the viewpoint of the NPIA. After the stockholders' meeting, SOHIO held a press conference. Curtiss said:

> In effect, what I said was, 'How would you feel if you were trying
> to conduct the business of a company and that business was dis-
> rupted by a horde who had gained illegal access to the meeting,
> but had no intention other than causing trouble?' [20]

Harry Fagan returned from vacation to face a deluge of phone messages and complaints about the shutdown of the stockholders meeting. On May 6, he issued a blistering memo to the Ohio Training Center and the NPIA groups about the events of April 22.

It was a full-blown dressing down. First, Fagan reiterated that the plan for the stockholders' meeting had been run by him, and that he had cautioned the groups to keep public opinion on their side and focus on preparations for negotiations.

In a favorite point that Fagan would bring up time and again in his dealings with the groups, he cautioned them to distinguish "...the difference between those who are committed to social change and those who participate in social therapeutic activities." [21]

He faulted the groups for losing public sympathy, for doing nothing to interpret the actions to the broader community, for exposing themselves to funding cutoffs from foundations and corporate donors, for bad research, and for alienating leadership that could split the coalition. He ended the list with the accusation, "...and worse than apparently having no clearly designed immediate next step or follow-up strategy, is the clear reality that I think you were used." Used, in his opinion, by NPA leaders.

He continued his memo by focusing his anger at NPA:

> My conclusion is simply [that] you lost in Cleveland, but NPA may well have won nationally, meaning I think NPA's national negotiating strategy for funding and programs is greatly enhanced through local skirmishes, but I would be hard pressed to enumerate the economic, political, or social negotiating points that are now better here in Cleveland. [23]

He expressed fear that NPIA was becoming an appendage of NPA.

Fagan stated his disappointment with lessons from the past not learned: "More to the point, though, is my chagrin in being unable to reconcile your collective organizing experience with these short-sighted tactics." [24] Then he closed with: "You must know that I feel a strong bond with you all in our common struggle. I leave it up to you to determine if and how you wish to deal with my concerns." [25]

Trapp claimed that the initiative for all the SOHIO actions came from the local groups, not from Chicago, as Fagan and SOHIO suspected. He said NPA played an advisory role, but that the local Cleveland groups were in the driver's seat. For NPA to be calling the shots from Conspiracy Central in Chicago was nonsense. Initiatives that NPA worked on came from the grassroots. [26]

Fagan's letter was not the only one the groups received. Another letter had gone out two days after the stockholders meeting from Tom Gannon, who at the time was a trainer for the Catholic Commission. Its tone was more sympathetic, but still critical.

The first point Gannon made was that SOHIO might come out of the event with public sympathy because disrupting other people's meetings violated many deeply held American notions of fair play and respect for free speech. He wrote:

> The disruption of the stockholders meeting after only five minutes has struck some of our supporters as unfair and unnecessary. As incredible as it seems, people still worry about such notions as "fair play" and "free speech," even during these days of Reaganomics and blatant corporate greed. [27]

Gannon continued in what is really more an essay, than a memo to the groups. He made an analogy between the situation NPIA was in, guerrilla warfare, and the importance of maintaining community support.

> As [is] so often seen in national liberation struggles, the small guerrilla forces gather public support and sympathy, gaining recruits and financial sustenance from the people while simultaneously isolating the government or the enemy from the masses. After such a campaign (if successful), the power structure gives in, not because it will suffer ultimate defeat, but because it loses the will or feels it is not worth continuing the battle. Small and large victories have been won [in] this way. [28]

Gannon worried that SOHIO would launch an effort to get the groups de-funded, and expressed the hope that if it did, it would be so clumsy and heavy handed that it would backfire. He feared that hits such as that made at the stockholders meeting portrayed the groups as illegitimate and extremist. Gannon also worried that the groups were in a tactical rut of using confrontation tactics that were not well thought out, that were predictable and that would be vulnerable to new responses from their opponents. To Gannon, they were using tactics to express anger, not linking them with the goal of negotiations or a longer-term strategy.

Gannon asked what the groups would do for encores after going to Alton Whitehouse's residence, and then breaking up the stockholders meeting. What measures were held in reserve? Gannon also feared such tactics would strengthen the resolve of SOHIO: "I've often found that a person will give in if he or she fears you, but never if he or she hates you." [29]

He encouraged them to lighten up a bit, break the tension, give SOHIO an opportunity to de-escalate, and give NPIA a chance to refocus public attention on the issues, rather than on its tactics of civil disobedience.

As had Fagan, Gannon ended his essay with an affirmation of support and solidarity with the groups: "I write this memo with trepidation because I don't want to come off the wrong way. I have a lot of respect for you all as organizers and as people." [30]

Responding to the criticism, George Barany of the Ohio Training Center sent a letter on behalf of NPIA dated May 8. Whether it was a response to Fagan or whether their letters had crossed in the mail is unknown. The one-page letter was no match for the polemics of Fagan and Gannon; it was a bare-bones restatement of what the campaign was about and an appeal to continue the support. The tone of the letter was that of a campaign on the defensive, if not yet under siege. Barany stated:

> Our actions are very similar to those of a union fighting for better working conditions. We are a union of Ohio community people try-

ing to pressure the sixth-largest U.S. energy producer to set up a program that would have a positive impact on our devastated state.[31]

He restated the dire condition of the state of Ohio in the midst of a budget deficit and the second-highest unemployment rate in the country:

> Please continue to support our efforts. Dramatic actions have to take place to make SOHIO realize the devastating effect their company policies are having on Ohio's population. Please call to find out what you can do to stop gas bills from rising. [32]

The campaign revealed the conflict between NPIA and its old mentor, Fagan. Barany described the rift:

> Fagan really didn't want us to do this stuff, but we laid out the option to people and people said let's go get them. The stockholders' meeting came after years of attempting to get somebody to seriously negotiate with us. The heat came down from SOHIO because they were a major contributor to Catholic Charities.

Barany felt that events such as the stockholders meeting jeopardized Fagan's status as the figurehead of the neighborhood movement. He said:

> The heat really came down and Fagan was kicked by the bishop: 'How could you allow this to happen?' He (Fagan) had no control. But basically, what he scolded us all for was that he puts his reputation on the line, he put his name out there promoting us, and how could we do this to him? We didn't do anything to him, but that's how he perceived it.[33]

On June 2, there was a meeting on SOHIO attended by Fagan and key organizers and leaders of the NPIA organizations. On June 3, Fagan sent a conciliatory, upbeat memo on the outcome of the meeting. He first apologized for the negative tone of his May 6 memo, then reaffirmed his respect for the role of neighborhood leadership, pledging to communicate with leaders and staff. Fagan pledged continued support of the commission for the groups, stating, "Please be assured that my life and the commission's existence are inextricably connected to the survival and growth of Cleveland's neighborhood movement" [34] He outlined how the following topics had been discussed in a strategy session: "Media emphasis and control, public opinion importance, internal organization communication, interpretation of continuity and follow up steps, and connectedness to neighborhood development entities." [35] The upbeat mood of the letter continued, backing away from the harsh criticisms of the May 6 memo: "...I see your strategy as well thought out and clearly focused;" "Your rationale for involvement in NPA was solid and your invitation to Gail was certainly misinterpreted by me," and "As far as institutional cover goes, I will continue to do what needs to be done to hold things together."

He ended the letter, "Obviously, the past is behind us, but I feel so much better about moving into the future together." [36]

While the initial blow-up over the stockholders meeting was past, it was apparent that the neighborhood groups were moving in directions of which Fagan was critical. Fagan perceived a lack of long-range strategic thinking and unrealistic notions of what it would take to win in issues such as SOHIO. The challenge, he believed, was to insure the survival of the groups, and the maintenance of their ties to the neighborhoods with issues that were not as glamorous as chasing Alton Whitehouse around town.

In an interview in 1983, as he was preparing to leave the commission for another position in New York, Fagan commented that watching the groups was like watching your twenty-year-old child who had just left home. You might not like what he is doing with his life, but there is not much you can do about it, either.

The groups not only got into trouble with the Catholic Commission, but also with their own neighborhoods. Gloria Aron of NWNIA and Kathy Jaksic of the SCSC faced criticism by their constituencies.

In St. Clair, the fallout from the stockholders meeting resulted in an emergency board of trustees meeting. Issues were brought up of who should have a say in such actions: the issues committee or the full board. Local companies that had supported SCSC in the past had to be mollified and met with. One of the most significant fallouts of the SOHIO campaign and this particular action for SCSC was a growing alienation between SCSC and the Ohio Training Center.

According to St. Clair leader Ron Jaksic, SCSC was initially suspicious of OTC at the time it was formed. These doubts and suspicions were common among the groups, and were to be as destructive as were any responses to the SOHIO campaign from the corporations of Cleveland. That suspicion grew under the pressure cooker of the SOHIO campaign. Jaksic recalled:

> When they were going to form the Ohio Training Center, there was a little bit of a rumble in the ranks. It was supposed to do the training and assist with leadership development. It was viewed by me as a formalization of the staff component. We knew that anything from the organization was a combination of staff direction and leadership. It was negative: too much strength, [too much] power for the staff. To me, [it was] manipulative of the leadership. [37]

Wesley Walker had been an organizer for Union Miles Community Coalition and was preparing to leave the Ohio Training Center at the time of the SOHIO campaign. He shared a common complaint that the SOHIO campaign strategy was all thunder and lightning and was without much substance.

According to Walker, the goal of George Barany, who had taken over OTC from Joe Mariano, was to produce as many people as possible for actions and events: "chair covers" in organizer lingo. People were being put on buses who did not know why they were there. They were participating in events and actions they did not understand, but did so out of personal loyalty to organizers and leaders they trusted. At any one event, there might be just one or two people who understood the issues. [38]

Buckeye archives do not comment much on local activities during the summer of 1982. Those items that are present show continued work on lobbying against decontrol of natural gas. This was the calm before the storm.

Coming Cleveland's way was NPA's Reclaim America campaign, a nationwide demonstration on wheels starting in Chicago with the ultimate destination being Washington D.C. and Wall Street. Reclaim America was NPA's response to the domestic policies of the Reagan administration. Shel Trapp said the idea came about at a leadership strategy meeting in Chicago. He thought it was a great idea.

Reclaim America ended up being a lot of fun, but, according to Trapp, it accomplished nothing.[39] It also set the stage for the one event that is most commonly identified as the beginning of the end of this era of community organizing in Cleveland – the Hunt Club hit.

Various groups in Cleveland prepared the way for the NPA caravan by garnering endorsements for the goals of Reclaim American Week. Included on the list was a proclamation from Cleveland city council welcoming Reclaim America and winning the support of Cleveland's Republican mayor, George Voinovich. Eileen Kelly, an organizer and future director of Near West Neighbors In Action, recalled the event:

> I remember Near West's part was to redo the Bill of Rights. They actually let us hang it [the banner] from the second floor of City Hall. I remember doing that on my mother's dining room table. It was the neighborhood Bill of Rights, so it was talking about all the things that are issues for neighborhoods. [40]

The Reclaim America caravan stopped at various cities on the way to Cleveland, picking up delegations from local affiliates along the way. They arrived in Cleveland September 12, 1982, for a rally in front of City Hall. By this time, the caravan was made up of eleven buses, including delegations from Cleveland that were to continue with the caravan on to its final destination.

As the rally ended on a brilliant autumn day, the call went out that it would be a good idea for the caravan to join the hunt for Alton Whitehouse, who was reported to be at the Chagrin Valley Hunt Club.

Located in exclusive Gates Mills, the Hunt Club was one of the most prominent social institutions of Cleveland's elite. If NPA and its affiliated groups in Cleveland wanted a confrontation with that elite, no better site could be found. Kelly said:

> We got on a bus and went out to Chagrin. We didn't know what the hell we were doing there. I mean, no one knew. Alton Whitehouse, are you sure he's going to be there? I remember somebody saying, 'What makes you think he's going to be here?'

The reports on whose idea it was to go to the Hunt Club are vague. The preponderance of opinion points to NPA leaders Cincotta and Trapp as initiators of the move, a role that Trapp denies.

With enthusiastic chants of "Freeze SOHIO, not Ohio", and people singing, "Give Us a Billion Dollars" to the tune of "Wade in the Water," the crowd was primed and needed little encouragement. It piled onto the buses and a rag-tag fleet of vans and private cars, and headed to the Hunt Club. Key staff and leaders were motivated by their unabashed hero worship of Cincotta and Trapp, the people who had inspired and trained them. How could they go wrong?

This awe can be seen in the words of Marlene Weslian of Citizens to Bring Broadway Back:

> (Gale Cincotta/ Shel Trapp) was the person to admire and to strive to be like, and who certainly knew everything about everything. The fact that NPA wanted to make Cleveland the stop and take part in this issue with us got people incredibly psyched up. [41]

What occurred when the 600 demonstrators landed at the Hunt Club was not just a political event. It was a collision of worlds that barely recognized each other's existence, and that never came into contact. That afternoon at the Hunt Club, the club chairman's Saturday lunch was in progress. The veranda was full of well dressed diners while on the grounds, members in English riding outfits were tending their mounts, gathering for the afternoon's equestrian events.

Pouring out of the buses were organizers in jeans and working-class and poor people in polyester. The Hunt Club had never before seen so many African-Americans or so many who were not among those the English call "the great and the good". As Marlene Weslian of CBBB remembered, "How dramatic to see the difference in how people live. .... It was so clear who had it and who didn't when you went there." [42]

A confrontation soon developed between the management of the Hunt Club, the overwhelmed police force of the village of Gates Mills, and the leadership of the demonstration. Weslian recalled the shock of those on the veranda,

Those poor people just didn't know what was going on. There they were sitting there having lunch, totally decked out, with tablecloths and crystal. People were saying 'Excuse me, I'm thirsty. Do you mind if I drink out of your water glass?' People literally didn't know what to do. [43]

The demonstrators demanded to see Whitehouse. Hunt club management responded that he was not present that day. Shouting matches between enraged luncheon guests and individual demonstrators erupted. The wife of James Lipscomb of the Gund Foundation reportedly had one person from the caravan take her glass of wine, toast her, and down it.

Finally, management of the club promised to give Whitehouse a message, and the demonstration ended. The caravan went on to its next stop, and the rest of the Cleveland contingent returned to face a reaction that made that of the stockholders' meeting seem tame.

While many who attended this hit were thrilled at the confrontation, there was also an undercurrent of embarrassment. Kelly remembered that:

It felt bad. It was no big fun thing. I remember some folks who went up on the porch. I remember other people saying, 'I'm glad I didn't go up there.' It was an embarrassing thing, very embarrassing for the Near West people. I think Gloria (Aron) felt a little bit thrilled by it, in retrospect, she was embarrassed. [44]

There was nothing embarrassing about it to Weslian:

When we went to the Hunt Club that day, that was the most incredible action we had ever done. I mean, we had done some incredible things in Washington over the years with NPA. We had gone to federal departments. We took over the Federal Reserve Bank, but going to the Hunt Club in Cleveland was really the pinnacle for Cleveland groups.

At a basic level, the action enraged the upper class of Cleveland beyond any other action the groups had taken. Mike O'Brien of NWNIA, explained that the hit had violated a norm more profound than the Constitution. "You do not embarrass the rich, among their rich peers." [45]

Again, a major concern of SOHIO was the position of the Cleveland media regarding the issue. What annoyed Curtiss was the behavior of the media during the Hunt Club action:

Two or three busloads descended on the Hunt Club seeking Al Whitehouse. They were persuaded to leave, but one thing we knew in the aftermath was that there was a TV camera on one of the buses. [46]

Curtiss made his anger apparent to Cleveland media:

> I was frankly very upset that a television camera and reporter had
> traveled with the group. That was totally unprofessional. It made it
> appear that this was perhaps a liberal journalist hand-in-hand. [47]

The action was roundly denounced in the media. The Village of Gates Mills
was so traumatized by the event that the village council met in emergency session to
listen to the outrage of its residents and to consider measures to ensure that nothing
of the sort would happen again.

SOHIO did not take the attacks sitting down. Curtiss made the rounds to the
foundations, and organizations supporting the groups. Surprisingly enough, the
Hunt Club was not the last straw, as far as SOHIO was concerned; it was the dis-
ruption of a speech that Whitehouse was scheduled to give at the Heights Area
Chamber of Commerce following the Hunt Club hit.

A busload of demonstrators from NPIA showed up, a confrontation ensued
and, according to Curtiss, one bystander was injured. As Curtiss recounted, "That
was the straw that really caused us to take steps to be sure that the usual funding
organizations in the city knew what these groups were doing. Whether they were
defunded, I don't know." [48]

Curtiss contacted Bishop Pilla, as he remembered:

> Somehow, we became aware that Catholic Charities might be
> involved in the funding of this activity. We went to the IRS to get
> copies, public information. It was important to us that community
> leaders understood what this organization was doing, how totally
> unrealistic they had become, how aggressive their actions were
> becoming. [49]

He also met with Dan Berry of the Gund Foundation.

> I don't recall the specifics of the conversation, but I do recall taking
> the position that what we were dealing with is a group that thinks
> this is the way to make progress. This is my feeling: If you give in
> you're going to get more of the same. SOHIO's point was, 'We're
> not interested.' There has been enough damage already that we're
> not interested in working with these people. When you looked at
> the people who were engaged in these demonstrations, they
> thought this was good fun. Let's be disruptive. When children get
> disruptive, you don't give in to them. [50]

Behind the scenes, according to some reports, a decision was made that the
Ohio Training Center (OTC) would take the fall for the action. It was defunded

and went out of business. The Hunt Club hit was considered the event that resulted in the defunding of community organizing in Cleveland. With the rise of the more docile, reasonable development corporations, funders had a way to stay involved in the neighborhoods without being linked to the wild and woolly organizing groups.

The attitudes of participants in the action at the Hunt Club, in retrospect, vary greatly. Many agree that it certainly was one of the most memorable hits and thought it was fun. Some look upon it as a youthful indiscretion, and there are those who considered it to be a demonstration of the power of the movement at this particular time. The powerful in Cleveland were starting to worry about the power of the neighborhood movement, according to this narrative.

One of the most remarkable admissions concerning the backlash against the groups came from Trapp, who said that NTIC and NPA underestimated the reaction and the power of SOHIO to make life difficult for the groups with the funders.[51]

Ken Esposito, formerly of Union Miles, who at the time of the Hunt Club hit was at the OTC, felt that the SOHIO campaign was an example of the groups overreaching. They became embroiled in a campaign, the repercussions of which they had not foreseen and that were to be disastrous for the movement.[52]

Many others, such as Gannon and Fagan, were not so convinced of the virtue of the action. They felt that the action had been decided on the spur of the moment by the training center and NPA. Many participants felt that there was little forethought about the action, what it would cost, and how they were to respond to the flak that would result from it. In short, they threw away the rulebook that they had followed – or were supposed to have followed. According to Weslian:

> It was the demise of organizing after that. God, did the shit hit the fan after that action, but, boy, was it incredible! I think that just shows how powerful the organizations had become and the fact that there wasn't anything we wouldn't do... It wasn't like going up to city hall. Supposedly the people are supposed to have a right to go to city hall. When you start going to people like the Hunt Club, that's where they drew the line.[53]

For all the suspicions, second thoughts, and disagreements about particular events or actions, the loyalty of the leadership to the overall campaign was solid, and is still defended to this day.

While those who remained in Cleveland caught the first wave of the backlash for the event, the Reclaim America caravan continued on to one of its major destinations, a rally on Wall Street with a planned hit at the stock exchange. Kelly described the event:

> We went to New York. We had a big parade, marched down Wall Street. Everybody had their Reclaim America signs. It was about neighborhoods. At the George Washington monument, they had

speeches about neighborhoods. It was fun; however, the big idea, like they conjured up with the Hunt Club, was to close the stock exchange. However, it was closed. We had all these people ready to go in, and it was closed, so people were pissed. [54]

The stock exchange was closed for a holiday, a minor detail that had escaped planners.

The rest of the trip, in Kelly's eyes, continued to be a mixture of the inspiring and the absurd. Events at Washington were inspiring. Then there was a hit in Philadelphia where they got lost and no one knew what they were doing. The ordeal of it led to Kelly and Aron fleeing to a cab and a lobster dinner. "We ran. We felt like we were escaping. We ran, got in a cab, and ate like pigs," [55] Kelly remembered.

The campaign after the Hunt Club hit went from the offensive to the defensive. In energy organizing meetings after the September hit, the goal of getting $1 billion from SOHIO was dropped, to the relief of almost everyone. Organizing around energy issues returned to pushing for modest reforms from East Ohio and the details of doomed legislation before Congress opposing deregulation that began with the Natural Gas Policy Act.

In organizing, your next great event is always in the pipeline, and the groups were undaunted in their planning. They brought up the idea of having a neighborhood tour, where they would have an opportunity to show representatives from East Ohio, SOHIO, and political, religious, and social service leaders what the implications of deregulation would be in the neighborhoods of Cleveland. The problem was that the campaign was trying to be nice to people they had spent the past year attacking. No one was interested in attending.

They also found that they had no more tricks up their sleeves in the aftermath of the past year's high-profile hits. A retreat was held in December 1982 by the major groups to evaluate where they were at the end of one of their stormiest years. Although no minutes or records have been found of that meeting, it is hard to see how it could have been upbeat. The warning that Gannon had made in the spring after the stockholders hit had been vindicated. They were out of ammo. There was no reason for anyone to pay attention to them any longer, and no one did. Many had told themselves that the SOHIO campaign was a demonstration of the power of the movement. Instead, it represented its bankruptcy.

As bad as the SOHIO campaign proved for the groups, it was a boon for neighborhood weatherization programs. SOHIO, joined by East Ohio, flooded the neighborhoods with funding for energy audits and assorted weatherization programs.

East Ohio and SOHIO learned how easy it was to co-opt the opposition. It was hard to make the case that they were just thieving corporate bandits in light of this generosity. They finally won deregulation. The climate changed. Prices moderated, and the energy crisis was retired to the nostalgia of the 1970s, along with leisure suits, discos and community organizing.

Part 3

The Decline of Community Organizing in Cleveland

Chapter 9

The Movement Unravels

When you think about the movements that were around then, civil rights, peace, and the beginnings of the women's movement, the farm workers' movement, there were so many kinds of causes... You could get yourself into something other than the movies. I noticed when I first got into this business, kids would walk in, would have a hope, and would want to go to work. They had a certain intensity about their lives. Today, a kid comes out of Wooster College and says, 'I did this paper on Alinsky, and I either want to go into retailing or organizing.' There's no passion. [1]

Harry Fagan, *Commission on Catholic Community Action*

The community organizing movement that swept Cleveland's neighborhoods benefited from a unique set of favorable conditions, including the movement legacies of the 1960s, an available labor pool of potential organizers, obtuse and blundering institutions that were dream targets, institutional cover from the Catholic church, and funding from the federal government, the Gund Foundation, and the Campaign for Human Development. There was the synergy of the right people being at the right place at the right time in key institutions.

Many of the changes that helped to bring down the movement began with the election of President Ronald Reagan in 1980. The 1980s were dominated politically, socially, economically and culturally by a grand campaign to roll back twenty years of social change. The goal was to restore order by restoring public passivity and the traditional hierarchies of power in the family, at work, in schools, and in the public life of the nation.

This campaign to restore order was expressed locally in the overthrow of the

Kucinich administration and the drive to exorcise from public life in Cleveland anything that even hinted of the populism and insurgency it symbolized. Although the community organizations didn't like Kucinich either, their rabble-rousing tactics, irreverence towards authority, and grassroots values were not far enough removed from those of Kucinich to afford them safety. A top-down, consensus style of politics of –"go along to get along"– carried the day. The decline and fall of community organizing in Cleveland fit neatly into the overall themes of the post-Kucinich era.

This transformation occurred on many fronts. Foundations turned away from organizing and toward development. With the decline of unrest in the African-American community and the incorporation of that community's leadership into the establishment, the corporate elite did not feel a need to back organizing as riot insurance. With the restoration of political stability after the overthrow of the Kucinich administration, the corporations returned to their usual job of profit and gain.

On college campuses, idealism was out; business administration degrees were in. The steady supply of recruits for organizing positions dried up. The generation of organizers who had built the neighborhood groups left the profession driven by the pressures of marriage, family, and the need for a saner, more secure way of life. Many, if not most, migrated with the funding opportunities into the burgeoning world of the new development corporations. Others left organizing altogether. City hall learned how to deal with the neighborhoods. A new generation of city council members, many with neighborhood activist experience, found their footing and asserted their hold on their wards by turning development corporations into new and improved reincarnations of the old ward organizations.

Of the original staff of the Catholic Commission who had helped launch the movement, none were still around. Dan Reidy left the priesthood and moved to San Francisco to become an attorney. Harry Fagan left in 1983 to work for the Center for Pastoral Life in New York City, where he died of cancer in 1992. His mentor, William Cosgrove, took a new assignment in East St. Louis, Illinois, and retired in ill health. He died within a month of Fagan. Bishop James Hickey became James Cardinal Hickey in Washington D.C.

An autopsy of this era of activism in Cleveland, would find a multitude of wounds that, taken individually, would not have killed the movement, but, taken together, were fatal.

The Commission Backs Away

One of the most significant developments was the withdrawal of the Catholic Commission from active involvement in the movement. The start of this process dates from the spinoff of the Ohio Training Center (OTC) from the Catholic Commission in 1980.

In one respect, it was a natural separation. The community organizations were no longer projects of the commission, but were fully autonomous organizations with their own administration, decision-making bodies, and fund-raising arms. They chafed under what they perceived to be the commission's paternalism, particularly that of Fagan. Tom Gannon recalled an article in the Plain Dealer that gave Fagan a huge spread. While no one could doubt Fagan's contributions, many in the neighborhoods were put off by the publicity, which Gannon felt Fagan reveled in. The article suggested Fagan had done it all by himself, when the movement was far broader and deeper than any one person. One of Gannon's and Joe Mariano's motivations for founding the training center was to enable the movement to leave home, the home of Harry Fagan. [2]

According to Joe Garcia, who was a member of the commission's board in the early 1980s, a marked change in the attitude of the diocese towards the groups and the commission occurred with the installation of Bishop Anthony Pilla in January 1981. Under Bishops Issenmann and Hickey, the commission had a lot of latitude. This relative autonomy ended under Pilla, who saw the commission as a part of the Diocese of Cleveland, and accountable to him.

Pilla was an unusual choice for bishop because Cleveland was his home. The general rule for appointing bishops was to bring in a bishop from out of town. James Hickey was not on a first-name basis with the movers and shakers of Cleveland who were regularly trashed by the groups. Pilla had had a long and distinguished career in Cleveland, and knew many of these people. It made him much less sympathetic to those who portrayed them as public enemies. [3]

While Gannon felt that Pilla's familiarity with the elite chilled the atmosphere for confrontational organizing, Len Calabrese, present-day director of the Catholic Commission, saw Pilla's hometown heritage as an asset. It made him more knowledgeable and sensitive to the concerns of the parish grassroots. [4]

Many who were close to the Catholic Commission such as Garcia, felt that the change in attitude by the diocese was rationalized by a study the Gund Foundation commissioned of the community organizations, begun by Art Bloom of the Case Western University's School of Applied Social Science (SASS) and finished by Michael Murphy, also of SASS. Garcia, who was on the commission board, felt the study was taken at the initiative of the diocese, but Gannon remembered it originating earlier at the suggestion of the Gund Foundation. Garcia considered the study to be a test that the community groups were destined to fail, giving the diocese an excuse to withdraw from community organizing. According to Garcia, the community organizations came out of the Murphy report looking like a mess, although Gannon remembered the report being not all that bad. Garcia thought the study used absurd criteria to judge community organizing:

> When you do organizing, this is a creative event. These are artists who work on intuition, response, timing, and getting ideas at 2:30 in the morning. They don't act in the confines of a bureaucracy or an organization. Forget about it! It's like taking a duck out of

water. Murphy says, 'Eh, this organization is not efficient.' All this management garbage. You can't organize, you can't tell Picasso to come in at 8, go home at 4. You know and get what Picasso creates for the world. [5]

It is interesting that Murphy was chosen for the task. His wife had been hit by Citizens to Bring Broadway Back at a meeting when she represented her employer, Forest City Enterprises, before the group. Murphy did not like community organizing, and he was furious over the hit. It is hard to see how any study he led could have been objective, yet the report was a success because it justified a major shift in the commission's attitude toward the groups. From the time of the study onward the impetus for organizing shifted to the parishes.

Garcia was livid, and confronted Fagan at a commission event:

So I ripped. Harry, in his mightier-than-thou rhetoric said 'Joe, it's a strategic decision that we will now get organizing out of the parish council.' I said to him, 'You gotta be kidding me!' He said, 'Joe, we'll be able to spread organizing wider throughout the diocese by turning over this portfolio of organizing to the parish council.' He said it with a straight face! I looked at him and said, 'You gotta be kidding me,' I mean, I was laughing and angry, and he was so good at what he did. He didn't blush.... It was a great performance. I said, 'Harry you're in the wrong business. Go to Hollywood, Harry. Go to Broadway, Harry.' The relationship was not the same after that between him and me.[6]

Len Calabrese of the commission looked upon the diocese's disengagement with community organizing as a reflection of changing times and a response to outside pressures on the diocese, not as a repudiation of organizing, activism, or advocacy.

The incentive to change came in the advent of the Reagan administration. Its bellicose foreign policy and hostility toward the American welfare state shifted the focus of all Catholic activists to issues of peace and poverty. By 1983, the National Council of Catholic Bishops was issuing major statements on the economy and peace.

The challenge for the American church was how to mobilize around these issues, and the solution was to turn back to the parishes to mobilize the Catholic constituency. In addition unease was stirring in some parishes about the activities of the groups and the loss of some of their best people to the groups.[7]

Withdrawal of the commission removed much of the political cover that the groups had enjoyed since the mid-1970s at a time when the national political and social climates were shifting dramatically to the right.

Funding

> Where are you going to get money for organizing? As I said, you can get a list
> of volunteers to activate the program. The people who were the staffs of these
> organizations worked for pennies. With the exception of a few enlightened
> neighborhood businesses, where are you going to get the money? You just
> aren't.[8]
>
> Hank Doll, *George Gund Foundation*

Funding helped to create the environment in which organizing flourished, and
its withdrawal dramatically altered that environment. The Catholic Commission
under Fagan helped open sources of funding through the Campaign for Human
Development and the Gund Foundation. The groups were also funded by grants
from the Law Enforcement Assistance Administration (LEAA) and the Federal
Emergency Management Agency (FEMA), and they were staffed by subsidized
volunteers from the VISTA program.

Community organizations in Cleveland started experiencing financial decline in
the early 1980s. With or without foundation reaction to the SOHIO campaign,
funding would have run out sooner, rather than later. First, the funding from the
foundations was limited to three-year funding cycles. By the early 1980s, the funding cycles and extensions of those cycles began to run out. Second, the organizations were badly hit by the arrival of the Reagan administration. Ken Esposito of the
Ohio Training Center was called on inauguration day 1981 by the new head of the
Federal Emergency Management Administration (FEMA) and was told to stop
operations immediately on the program he was running. When asked why, the official was blunt: "Because we are in power now, and you are out." [9]

One of the worst blows came with the curbing of the VISTA program, which
provided vital organizing staff. The involvement of VISTA volunteers in advocacy
organizing had enraged conservatives for years. They made gutting the program part
of their "de-fund the left" campaign. This can be seen in the letter Sandra Kluk of
Buckeye Woodland Community Congress (BWCC) received from Ted Wysocki of
the National Training and Information Center (NTIC), their technical assistance
agency for VISTA, on April 21, 1981:

> Needless to say, it does not look very good for any of you getting
> VISTAs next year. The new guidelines for VISTAs state that they
> don't want VISTAs organizing 'angry people' (maybe you want to
> try polite people for a change). Two issues they mention for
> VISTAs to work on next year are youth and energy (meaning train-
> ing people to actually weatherize their homes, not fighting rate
> increases).[10]

One delusion shared by both funders and funded was the notion that organizing should become self-sufficient. Organizing was not like opening up a muffler

shop. A national leader of neighborhood activism, Monsignor Geno Baroni, never believed that neighborhood organizing could become self-sufficient. [11] Even Alinsky always had his hand out. However, little dissent from the officially stated goal of self-sufficiency was heard.

From the start, fundraising was on the agenda of the neighborhood groups. It was not a concern that appeared suddenly in the early 1980s as the foundations were backing out of the organizing scene.

On December 20, 1978, Jim Lipscomb, director of the Gund Foundation, wrote Fagan to announce the award of a second-year grant for the Training & Technical Assistance (T&TA) program. Lipscomb was especially interested in the financial future of the program and its attainment of self-sufficiency. The 1979 copies of the proposal belonging to the Gund Foundation were heavily marked in the section dealing with fundraising and financing, [12] demonstrating concern on the part of the foundation about the future financial viability of the movement. The foundation also was concerned about the move of the groups to a statewide organizing center, the Ohio Training Center. If funding self-sufficiency was daunting on the neighborhood level, how much more difficult would it be on the state level?

The most important withdrawal in funding, financially and symbolically, was made by the Gund Foundation. It was then, and still is, a prime arbiter of the direction non-profits take in Cleveland. Hank Doll, former program officer for the Gund Foundation, described the foundation's reasons for its pull-back from funding the organizing groups:

> Most projects that you put money into, [you do it] four or five
> years at the most, then you're done. The theory behind that is those
> organizations are going to finance themselves from other sources.
> They will have demonstrated their value by then, and other sources
> will be underwriting their activity or it will have made its contribu-
> tion. That's been the practice of foundations for a long time, not
> just Gund. So in our case, being with some of these things for nine
> years was a really long commitment. [13]

It was not only time that was running out for the groups. They were becoming a problem for the funders. What the foundations were looking for clashed with what the groups were interested in.

It is undeniable that the funding organizations of Cleveland preferred the well-behaved development groups to the often-outrageous community organizations. It is also clear that institutions such as foundations have long sought a form of democracy that will not inconvenience business. The history of citizen participation schemes shows how such institutions crave the legitimacy of grassroots organizations and find the transmission of information that they gain from the relationship useful, but they are not interested in losing control of the ability to frame and define issues before the public or of finding their interests challenged, both of which happen frequently when grassroots organizations begin to develop. They also had lost faith not only in the groups, but also in the quality of organizing advice and strategy that people were receiving from the Ohio Training Center, as was evident in the fallout from the SOHIO controversy. Gannon, who was watching the events from the sidelines at the commission, commented:

> You can defend good organizing because good organizing wins and good organizing makes sense and good organizing empowers people. Bad organizing doesn't always do that, and you can't defend that organizing. Therefore, when push comes to shove, if you don't believe in the product that you're funding, and you see some of the problems with it, you are certainly not going to take the heat for it.[14]

A common complaint was that the funding came too easily, was too dependent on just a few sources, and created a situation in which the constituencies of the organizations were passive recipients of services provided by the organizations. The rank-and-file were not expected to make an effort to fund the organizations from such sources as membership dues. Gannon cited his experience with the United Farm Workers. Caesar Chavez insisted that all members pay dues. When they paid dues, they invested in the union and showed their support. They had a crucial link with the organization. The communities of Cleveland were not affluent, but were not as poor as the farm workers of Delano, California. Yet the community organizations never expected from their members what any other organization does: dues regularly paid.[15]

Bill Callahan, an organizer for Citizen Action, felt that the blame for the financial vulnerability of the groups had to be laid at the feet of Fagan.

> Whatever role Harry may have played that was negative was the willingness to be Big Daddy in fundraising terms to organizations that were far more dependent on outside resources than they should have been. Harry raised the money. It probably looked like a terrific thing to do at the time he was doing it. They were so driven by outside considerations, whether it was what we can raise this year, or letting Chicago play such a big role in the agendas, everybody was dependent on an outside funder. Some of that can be traced back to Harry's over-willingness to be the good guy for everybody.[16]

The decline of secure funding sources created a dynamic that undermined the groups. Increasingly, emphasis was given to whatever fundraising schemes seemed even remotely promising.

Organizations began to raise funds with local businesses for neighborhood Yellow Pages directories. There was an attempt to launch a canvassing operation along the lines of Citizen Action. Organizations started to contract to provide services for city programs. On the Near West Side this involved a program to install smoke detectors in private homes.

Foundation grants for such programs were so tightly written that providing these services was all that was allowed. Organizing was explicitly forbidden. With the staff single-mindedly focused on scratching together financial survival, little time remained for the work of nurturing block clubs, developing leadership, and issues, and keeping in contact with peers in other parts of the city. Not only couldn't they sustain critical funding, but the desperate efforts to seek new sources of funding derailed their ability to maintain their very reason for existence, the organization and development of the people of the neighborhood.[17]

Burnout

It was such an intense period in my life. There was no way I could continue that pace for any longer than I did, actually. That's another problem with it: Nobody figured out how to maintain those original people or [find] the new ones to replace them. Maybe it was too intense. We put incredible burdens on ourselves. [18]

Marita Kavalec, *Union Miles Community Coalition*

Community organizing in Cleveland depended on a particular cadre of organizers, leaders, and activists. When they began to leave the scene, few, if any, replacements came to take their places. By the early to mid-1980s, staffing had reached a critical point and added to all the other problems bearing down on the groups.

Being a community organizer during the heyday of the groups could be an exhilarating way of life for a young idealist. You weren't just reading about the crucial issues of the day, you were dealing with them, personally, every day. You weren't just studying history in a college seminar, you were making history on the streets and in the communities of Cleveland.

The down side to this was miserable pay, grueling hours, and endless meetings, to say nothing of the drudgery of "door knocking". Enforcing these conditions was a movement ethos of self-sacrifice, where complaints about conditions elicited a response that questioned your dedication and commitment. Judy Opalach, an organizer for St. Clair Superior Coalition and Citizens to Bring Broadway Back, recalled the shocked reaction she received to her refusal to go to an event because she had made other plans. To this day, former leaders of these groups, comment on their sense of amazement at the dedication of the staff, at their willingness to soldier on with long hours and low pay, and how they would never wish that fate on others.

Community organizers were not the only ones used up by the process in Cleveland. So were community leaders. The great failure of the organizations of this era was that they did not develop new leaders to take over when older leaders pulled back or quit. It was easier to call on the old reliables than to find new leaders.

A process developed wherein people who were developed as leaders on one particular issue soon were tapped to be on the board of the organization on a personnel or finance committee or leading another issue committee. It was always a challenge to balance these duties with the normal demands and responsibilities of everyday life. People tired of the extra demands placed on them by the organization and either pulled back or dropped out altogether.

Barb Pertz described the process of burnout at BWCC:

> I was fortunate that I didn't have to contend with a husband who said, 'You're going to another meeting?' or children holding on to your skirt saying, 'Mommy, stay home tonight!' People were dedicated. They could start to see that things were changing. They wanted to be a part of that change. In Buckeye Woodland...people who were around in the beginning weren't at the end. Just like the organizers, they got burned out.[19]

It wasn't just a matter of burnout for the leaders. Everyday life was becoming more difficult in the 1980s. The earlier groups still operated in a world where many neighborhood housewives did not have to work outside the home or where many people were retired or were living on pensions. They had time to participate in community activities, and those activities were underwritten by Cleveland's traditional manufacturing sector.

The massive deindustrialization that hit Cleveland in the 1970s and 1980s saw the loss of more than 60,000 manufacturing jobs in Cuyahoga County from 1979 to 1983, a twenty six per cent decline in manufacturing jobs.[20]

These losses hit the areas organized by the groups and drastically changed family dynamics. In order to maintain their standard of living, many families had to have both adults working. Groups were forced to rely on fewer of their founding activists to volunteer for activities.[21] Many became single mothers, either from divorce or through the death of a spouse. Retired volunteers died or became incapacitated. Barb Pertz commented that a blow to BWCC was the dying off of all the little old Hungarian ladies who used to turn out for meetings and actions.

Product Over Process: The Rise of Development

The few groups that remain from the ones that existed originally exist more as service providers now than as organizing groups. It would be very difficult to sell to any of the foundations or to city government the concept of grassroots organizing. It is a failed concept. But, yes, the groups that do exist either exist as appendages of council people, and are often very supportive of the individual council people, or as appendages of the housing or development corporations that they once set up and controlled. [22]

Mike O'Brien, Near West Neighbors in Action

The community organizations of Cleveland gave birth to development corporations, that consolidated and ran programs that came from the mother organization's victories. With time, these development arms either replaced the parent organization or the parent organization transformed itself to fit the new development agenda.

A whole generation of community development non-profits, particularly housing corporations, was formed in the early 1980s. The Cleveland Housing Network was organized in 1981. The Near West Housing Corporation, a spinoff of Near West Neighbors in Action was begun in 1980. Union Miles Development Corporation, formed in 1981 as a subsidiary of Union Miles Community Coalition, absorbed its parent group in 1985. The Broadway Area Housing Coalition was formed in 1981 out of an earlier effort, called North Broadway Housing for Neighbors and Citizens to Bring Broadway Back. The St. Clair Superior Coalition helped found a housing group, COHAB, at about this time. In the Buckeye area, veterans of Buckeye Woodland Community Congress started Bank on Buckeye (BOB) and the Buckeye Evaluation and Training Institute (BETI), which served as a weatherization and housing rehab consulting organization.

National organizations, such as the Local Initiatives Support Corporation (LISC) and the Enterprise Foundation, began to build relationships with the new development groups. Finally, Norm Krumholz began the Center for Neighborhood Development (CND) at Cleveland State University to continue the advocacy planning that he had pioneered at the Cleveland City Planning Commission. As the infrastructure for organizing was collapsing, the infrastructure for development was burgeoning.

The development corporations rose to prominence, displacing the old community organizations for several reasons. They were product-oriented. If they succeeded with a program, there was something solid to show for the effort, usually a rehabbed house, salvaged apartment building, or a renewed shopping strip. This proved irresistible to funding sources. Brick-and-mortar accomplishments could be displayed in annual reports. Ribbon-cuttings could provide publicity and psychological strokes for bank representatives, politicians, and other public figures whose goodwill was invaluable. Such accomplishments also were nice to have on your resume if you were an up-and-coming director of a nonprofit.

Empowerment could not be photographed. Democracy could not be charted. How the process of working with a community organization helped a neighborhood person gain self-confidence, learn skills, change her life for the better, or broaden her view of the world could not be described statistically on a spreadsheet or boiled down to the bottom line.

A key to low-income housing development in Cleveland, as used by the non-profits, was tax-credit financing, in which private investors sheltered their income from taxation by investing in low-income housing ventures. The impact was not only financial, but also political: It sealed the alliance between the development corporations and the corporate community.[23]

The development corporations were safe entities to fund. Investors could be pretty sure that a local non-profit would be the last organization to disrupt a stockholders meeting, "roast" a bureaucrat or politician alive, or defeat a plan for a downtown development scheme. The development corporations fit ideally into the consensus-obsessed, don't-rock-the boat atmosphere of post-Kucinich Cleveland.

Development corporations put a premium on professionalism and the acquisition of technical expertise to carry the day. Their emphasis was not on developing the skills of neighborhood people or subjecting development plans to the slow, patient process of grassroots democratic decision making. Time was money. Negotiations could not be carried out in public. Deadlines had to be reached. Funders and investors would not wait. The grassroots became a passive cheering section for the technical virtuosity of the professionalized staff.

The Model Collapses

One of the most significant signs of a movement in decline was the collapse of Buckeye Woodland Community Congress, the organization that was a prototype of how to put together a community organization in Cleveland.

The organizations of the era did not just die on a precise date. The end most often came as the result of a long, painful illness. In the case of BWCC, the decline was from 1983 until it formally disbanded on December 29, 1987. During much of this time, it really did not exist as a viable organization. Those members who remained loyal were like the last residents of an abandoned city.

Buckeye began to come apart from financial pressures. A funding history of the organization showed a slow, relentless drying up of one financial well after another. The early years saw foundation funding from the Campaign for Human Development and the Cleveland Foundation. Important funding sources, such as VISTA, ended with the advent of the Reagan administration.

The financial burden then fell exclusively on private foundations. This effort faltered by early 1984. For the rest of the time, BWCC won one or two grants, but otherwise subsisted on handouts from its spinoff development corporations, Bank on Buckeye (BOB) and the Buckeye Evaluation and Training Institute (BETI), and increasingly desperate and improbable fundraising schemes.

Buckeye not only succumbed to the usual funding woes that plagued the rest of the groups; it also was racked by internal disputes that became more vicious under the pressure cooker of financial need.

Ironically, one of Buckeye's major accomplishments proved to be one of the flash points in its war with itself. In 1981, BWCC helped found a consortium of banks that would help fund housing rehab in the neighborhood. Called Bank on Buckeye (BOB), it and its sister group, BETI, soon began to eclipse the parent organization in funding and staff, sparking organizational and individual jealousy among those still active in BWCC.

The targets of the jealousy were Sharon Bryant and Pat Kinney, who had begun working for BOB. BOB and BETI not only had financing that BWCC lacked, they also had on their boards many former leaders of the BWCC. There was a dispute over office space. Buckeye could no longer afford its old office, and BOB offered it office space in the back of its offices. The leadership of BWCC was insulted. The acrimony went so far that a faction of BWCC actually picketed a BOB-sponsored neighborhood tour for a national economic development conference.

A good indicator of the health of an organization can be found in the minutes of its executive or governing boards. In the case of BWCC's executive board, the contrast between the minutes taken in the first five years of its existence and those of the middle 1980s is striking.

Minutes from the years between 1975 and 1980 are meticulous and comprehensive. The board disciplined itself; members were required to attend or to be excused; otherwise, they were asked to resign. BWCC's executive board was a working board, discussing committee reports and setting the direction of the congress on major issues.

By 1983, board minutes became fragmentary and, in many cases, are missing. The board no longer discussed issues on the agenda, but was increasingly obsessed with minute details of event planning and fundraising that, in an earlier time, would have been handled in subcommittees. Minutes no longer were typed, and were reduced from two to three single-spaced pages to one page. From 1985 until it disbanded at the end of 1987, the executive board of BWCC was the organization, with nothing under it to lead.

All of this coincided with the retirement or falling back of the old leadership: Diane Yambor, Sharon Bryant, Agnes Jackson, and Barbara Pertz. They were replaced by people who had always been active in BWCC, but who had only recently become interested in leadership. Leola Criswell, Jenette Terrill, Alma Cooper, and Lottie Person were among those who joined the board. George Barany, former BWCC organizer and executive director, came on board, as well. His tenure was brief, and he left totally exasperated by the experience. Executive director Sandra Kluk assessed the new board:

> They felt they should just control the organization, period. They
> didn't like the organizing of the congress. They didn't like the con-
> frontational attitude. They didn't like the white staff. They didn't
> like some of the black leaders.[24]

Kluk also was concerned about their failure to do the basic work needed to maintain the group. She described it:

> I tried to tell the leaders we haven't been organizing as much on the street because leaders used to go to street club meetings. People don't know you, and there were a lot of new people out there who haven't been to hits and actions. [We said,] 'They're going to be at the convention, and so you want to get out there and campaign.' [25]

One of the greatest sources of conflict was the new board president, Lottie Person, who assumed the office in 1984. The board minutes of June 21, 1984, contain the following:

> Earl Jefferson charged misconduct by Mrs. Person as president. [He] said [she] had not followed protocol and procedures, ignored sentiments of the other board members, and did not let the vice president know what was going on, thus undercutting his ability to perform if needed. He made a motion to ask her to resign. The motion [was] approved twenty to eight. [26]

The motion did not have any teeth. The next executive board meeting, held on July 19, 1984, included an entry that Mrs. Person announced that she intended to stay as president and that everyone should just try to get along. Getting along was not likely, given two areas of conflict on the board. The first was the entrance of local politics into board decisions. Many new board members were politically connected and began using the board to push the agenda of their particular party. Sharon Bryant described the entrance of politics into the board:

> We had the people from the 21st District Caucus (Louis Stokes's political organization). We had the Nagys from the Republican party. How can I benefit my party? What am I going to get out of it? [27]

The second flash point was racial. A failure of community organizing in Cleveland was its inability to recruit and keep African-American organizers and staff. With the exception of such organizers as Wess Wells, Larry Allen, and Greg Groves, the list of African-American organizers was very short. Within the increasingly vitriolic world of BWCC in its decline, this failure became a political football within the organization. Just as pressure was building from the board to hire African-American organizers, the ability of the organization to keep any staff at all was more in doubt each day. To make matters worse, prospective organizers who were hired often served the dual purpose of not only being organizers, but of being the eyes and ears of one or another faction on the board.

Another source of friction was the closed-door method of governing BOB and BETI. There was a deep suspicion of corruption and favoritism based on the funding of the new development groups.

Alma Cooper, one of the new leaders, did agree with Bryant on the character of board disputes. They were not about policy differences; they were battles based on personalities and factions. The battles were being fought against a backdrop of dwindling board participation. Cooper also blamed the old leadership for becoming too insular. She blamed the old leadership under Sharon Bryant for the unwillingness to work with the new board or to give up control of the organization. When they went over to the new development arms, they took their expertise and experience with them. No mechanism existed in the organization to maintain access to that expertise and experience. It was the personal property of those who possessed it and traveled with them, in many cases, to better things.[28]

The news of Buckeye's problems became official with two articles in the *Plain Dealer*. The first appeared on June 25, 1984; the second, on September 30, 1985. The 1984 article reflected Buckeye's demise from a seven-person staff and a $100,000 budget to director Sandra Kluk facing laying off herself and her last organizer just to pay the rent for the office. The invisibility and extinction of BWCC was guaranteed. As Sharon Bryant said in the *Plain Dealer*:

> 'We need the staff so we can develop our projects full time.' said Bryant. 'Time is the villain, because most of us in the organization work, and all we can really devote is evening time... If you don't organize, then you're not visible in the community, and people just don't know you're out there.'[29]

Lottie Person disappears from the archives after 1984, replaced by Leola Criswell. Criswell was a vice president of BWCC who had become active with the congress late in its life. Her main experience had been organizing block watches in her neighborhood.

Criswell was a controversial figure who was blamed by some of the old timers for helping sink the organization; however, the archives show that she was largely responsible for organizing the attempt to bring BWCC back in 1985. She took the helm of the organization and tried to keep it functioning, and was responsible for BWCC to the end.

The second article covered the effort to raise Buckeye from the dead. BWCC recalled a leader from better days, Ken Kovach, now a consultant on non-profit organizations, who was widely respected, regardless of faction. Kovach led a series of meetings and workshops to salvage BWCC.

The problems he found revolved around the quality of leadership and conflict between leaders wedded to the old days and leaders with limited knowledge of community organization, as well as staff becoming involved in internecine battles and money pressures. Kovach described the situation:

Some of the new leadership lacked the kinds of skills and a real orientation to what the organization was really about. They got plugged in through one little piece, and maybe never really saw a big picture. There was also tension among some of the old leaders who still lived there and who still wanted to be active and some of the new leadership who didn't like their style. I think a third point is that now there was money [with BOB and BETI] to do some things.[30]

At public meetings Kovach tried to rally the troops with appeals to the old spirit and the voluntary efforts that helped start Project Interface and BWCC. But appeals would not bring back the old days.

The end was a tragicomedy, with leaders stealing Rolodexes and records and changing locks on the office door while the landlord prepared to begin eviction proceedings for non-payment of rent.

Leola Criswell closed the office after the December 1987 board decision to formally disband. Whatever faults she may have had as a leader, she had a sense of the historical importance of BWCC and donated the organization's records to the Western Reserve Historical Society. So ended the Buckeye Woodland Community Congress.

In Search of the Smoking Gun

In human folklore, there are creation myths and end-of-the world myths. The community organizing movement in Cleveland was no exception. The most popular end of the world myth, among veterans of the movement, is that the movement had become a threat to the status quo. The powers that be responded by orchestrating a funding cut off that lead to the demise of the groups. This is a myth that plays into the rough-and-tough machismo of this time and flatters veterans of organizing into thinking that they had more power and were more threatening to the status quo than they ever were. It neatly absolves the groups, their organizers, and their leaders from responsibility for their own downfall.

Three factors make it difficult to confirm the case for an elite conspiracy against the groups. The first is the way that power is exercised. The process is a slowly rolling consensus reached in meetings without notes, in conversations at lunch or in a hallway, and in the myriad small signals that coalesce to establish new sets of rules and new lists of those who are in and those who are out of favor.

Lance Buhl, head of corporate giving for SOHIO, said that it would be hard to crack down on the groups and still fund neighborhood efforts because often the same people were involved. Buhl commented on the impact of the Hunt Club in Diana Tittle's history of the Cleveland Foundation, *Rebuilding Cleveland*. In his view, the hit put a permanent end to funding advocacy organizing, but not to the funding of neighborhood development.[31]

The second reason the smoking gun won't be found is that there is to this day, no consensus on what led to the end. Many veterans focus on the funding, others believe that a more complex set of reasons led to the decline of organizing.

The third reason is that, in the aftermath of the Hunt Club hit, many groups faltered and died; some did not. BWCC folded in 1987; UMCC closed in 1985. NWNIA finally went out of business around 1990 after a series of near-death experiences. CBBB was dissolved in 1993. St. Clair Superior Coalition was the last to give up its old organizational name and identity in 2001.

The names of those who remained may have been the same, but they could not resist the pull of the development agenda. Instead of being organizations that built campaigns based on issues coming from the grassroots, they became organizations that mobilized communities in support of development. They lived on in a world they helped create, but no longer recognized, understood, or influenced.

While the myth of an elite crackdown has its merits, it grossly oversimplifies the organizations' problems. The truth would include not only elite disfavor, but also many internal and external factors that, combined with elite reaction and shrinking social and political space for organizing, created a lethal environment for community organizations in Cleveland.

Tom Andrezjewski, neighborhood reporter for the *Plain Dealer*, explored the pressures coming down on the groups in two articles written in 1982 and 1985. In the first, titled *Budget Cut to Tone Down Activism Here?* Andrezjewski puts forth the issue:

> Activist community groups face the prospect of toning down their agenda for social and economic change and sticking to more prosaic projects, such as providing attic insulation or house paint in city neighborhoods.
>
> Cuts in federal programs, ranging from anti-crime dollars to housing programs, are forcing neighborhood groups to rely more on banks, corporations, and foundations for money. At least indirectly, and often directly, those are the targets of their protests.
>
> So far, no direct evidence exists that any organizations, even the ones which have participated in activities such as the lunchtime disruption at the Chagrin Valley Hunt Club last September, have been excluded from local philanthropy.
>
> But the people in charge of granting money to civic groups stress that funds are for constructive projects and not for organizing demonstrations for so-called systemic change.[32]

In the 1985 piece, Andrezjewski eulogizes the era he was instrumental in covering, touching on the issues of funds drying up, burnout, and competition from development corporations. He ends with this lament:

The problems remain. But how long will Cleveland's banks keep full-time 'neighborhoods' executives around, now that there is less and less pressure on them? How long will they respect the concept of inner city reinvestment?

And how long will it be before insurance companies once again start offering only partial coverage at high rates for home-owners in the city?

How long will it be before the mayor and councilmen do nothing but obtain city services and neighborhood improvements only for their cronies and political front groups? And no longer join community groups fighting powerful institutions that trample neighborhoods and neighborhood people?

One reason Cleveland declined so horrendously in the early 1970s was because of the very apathy that apparently has reappeared. Beginning in the 1960s, few cared about neighborhoods or the welfare of neighborhood people, not even they themselves. Our city almost fell apart from decay, racial tension and the Ralph Perk/George Forbes years at city hall.

Unless people in the city once again push hard to make themselves and their issues noticed, we'll all be headed for the same despair. [33]

Chapter 10

LEGACIES

Bottom line, it was the development corporations. That was the legacy. [1]

George Barany, *Buckeye Woodland Community Congress*

It may be a tiny thing, such as learning how to ask a question in public, or it may be a huge thing, such as standing up in front of a hundred people to make a speech. Those things change people's lives. That whole process of showing people that they have an impact makes a difference for the rest of their lives. I don't know the impact of the organization on the city, but on the people, it was huge. [2]

Eileen Kelly, *Near West Neighbors*

Community organizing's legacies continue to reverberate throughout the life of Cleveland. In many instances, these legacies show themselves in still-active institutions, programs, and ongoing projects. Many legacies are more personal, and are harder to track and describe. We see these legacies in individual lives that were changed forever by organizing, in informal networks of former activists, and in skills learned and taught to others. We will begin with the legacy of the movement as represented in the institutional geography of Cleveland's neighborhoods.

A Community Development Establishment

Cleveland today benefits from the presence of dozens of neighborhood-based development corporations working for housing and economic development. Many have come together in coalitions such as the Cleveland Housing Network. They are served by city wide support and funding organizations such as Neighborhood

Progress, Inc., The Local Initiatives Support Corporation, the Enterprise Foundation, and the Center for Neighborhood Development.

It is unlikely that the neighborhood development corporations and their supporting networks would have developed as they did without the earlier community organizing movement as their foundation. The organizing groups won the victories that the development groups consolidated and developed. They also won formal recognition of the value of neighborhoods, even if the major focus of post-Kucinich Cleveland has been on downtown development.

This legacy of a community development infrastructure of Cleveland is the consummation of one of the goals of the earliest founders of the movement. As Hank Doll of the Gund Foundation explained, the desire to empower people was not an end in itself when the Gund Foundation began its relationship with the Catholic Commission. The other goal was to use community organizing as a launch pad for successful development work in the neighborhoods. Since the 1950s, Cleveland had seen the failures of urban renewal and the Model Cities program. In the 1970s, organizing was perceived as a way to sustain neighborhoods and prepare them for development.

This time, there was some success. Neighborhoods defied formidable forces of poverty, crime, and unemployment to make advances in housing and business development. Inez Killingsworth, a leader of Union Miles Community Coalition, saw progress in her neighborhood:

> I see neighborhoods across the city being revitalized. I see lots of new construction. I see lots of rehab work happening. Lots of homes are being painted up because of that. I see people's gas and light bills getting paid because of the organized efforts we had. I see a better police-community relationship.[3]

Another veteran of UMCC, Hugh Kidd, commented,

> I think it gave people an opportunity to take a look at some of those problems and to do some positive things about it. I think that most of the development corporations have been effective in a number of areas, not only in trying to maintain the housing stock, but also in making banks aware that they were not making loans. And so now there are a number of banks who are making real efforts to come up with new programs so they can provide at least mortgage financing in the city of Cleveland.[4]

One of the greatest accomplishments was renewed investment in the neighborhoods by the financial industry. Not that it matched in any way the amount the financial industry had removed from the neighborhoods through redlining. Much of the bank activity was just glorified public relations. The financial industry still controlled lending policies. However, what investment was made was because of the use of the Community Reinvestment Act and the threat to use that act by community organizations that were determined to break open the closed doors of the Cleveland banking industry. Even if the early campaigns won scanty, partial victories, the work they did made it much easier for the city of Cleveland to make truly impressive breakthroughs in later years.

The long list of accomplishments, attainment of respectability, and creation of a community development establishment has had its downside, as well. The veterans of the old organizing groups often complain that the development sector doesn't recognize their contributions. As Frank Ford said:

> They don't even know it. Some of the staff people are totally oblivious of how they are benefiting from past organizing in how these banks treat them. They just don't understand.[5]

Killingsworth agreed:

> I don't think they understand or see the need to empower people. Their goals are just mainly to develop real estate. They don't do any other type of organizing. [6]

Failure to give the past its due blinds the development groups to the long-term harm of not having organizing going on in their neighborhoods. Without organizing, there are limited opportunities to discover and to develop new leaders to serve on boards and committees. The pipeline from the grassroots is shut down. The development corporations discovered that, without organizing, they were frequently flying blind in their own neighborhoods. An idea or a development project that looks wonderful at the board level might be viewed as the exact opposite on the street. Without organizers in contact with residents, the boards never know when they were about to step off a curb and get hit by a bus.

Changing Lives

Community organizing not only changed the city, it changed those who participated in it. Neighborhood residents, especially women who came from traditional blue-collar backgrounds, found a window on the world in the organization's activities. They met their peers from all over the country in conferences sponsored by National People's Action. They traveled to Washington, D.C., for the annual NPA convention. They gained knowledge from experts and authorities on issues of concern in their neighborhoods.

They also were exposed to fellow Clevelanders from across the racial divide. In one of the most segregated cities in the United States, the community organizing movement was an unprecedented example of interracial cooperation and action.

Neighborhood women learned how to run organizations, how to research issues, and how to speak in public, and gained enough confidence to be able to go toe-to-toe with members of the political and economic elite. They gained recognition for their work and their expertise, and their public and private lives would never be the same. The entire experience of working in the movement was an experience in personal education and development that was unavailable to them from any other source. Eileen Kelly of NWNIA described these changes:

> The successes were very personal in staff people, but mostly in the people you worked with in the neighborhoods. There was Gloria Aron, who became a different person. Not that she was terrible before, but she learned so much from being involved. She's still a force in her family and her immediate neighborhood. She is still able to accomplish things.

Kelly also saw how the process could backfire for the groups:

> Maggie Britton (a fellow organizer) and I used to joke that our biggest successes led to the downfall of the organization. Most of the single women with children felt empowered. They got jobs and left. It was self-defeating in that we were helping people, but it was hurting the organization. You teach people that they have control, or they find it. They do better for themselves. That's why I said it was very personal.[7]

Marita Kavalec saw much the same as Kelly had in how organizing changed the lives of individual people in the Union Miles neighborhood. She said:

> I think in terms of the individual people who never felt they could make a difference and who didn't think they had much to offer. That is the most significant thing. Dorothy Zeigler was a typical housewife and parent who didn't think she could do anything like speak in public, chair a meeting, write a speech, or say to the secretary of HUD what she thought. There were a lot of Dorothy Zeiglers in those communities. For me, that's what it was all about.[8]

Leaders and activists from the grassroots movement were not the only ones to benefit from the experience. One of the greatest legacies of the period has been that veterans of the era can now be found in responsible leadership positions throughout city government and in the non- profit world. Although fifteen to twenty years have passed since the end of this era, it is still common to find a stint of pounding the pavement as a block club organizer on resumes of leaders of Cleveland. George Barany, Norm Harrison, and Marita Kavalec were all organizers who felt they benefited from the experience.

> I think there are people around today who, like me, who went through those experiences who still are committed to doing this kind of work. It certainly was a learning experience that allowed some of us to move on to a more sophisticated level.[9]
>
> George Barany

> I'm very proud of the three-and-a-half years I spent in organizing. It helped me grow. I contributed to the community. I got some great skills and had real fun doing it. I have the opportunity from time to time to employ those skills and I have some basic skills I can utilize when confronted with a problem that requires organizing. Nothing intimidates me.[10]
>
> Norm Harrison

> Those of us who did this as a way of living, what we learned, how we grew up: We can still use it. I will appreciate it for the rest of my life.[11]
>
> Marita Kavalec

A More Democratic Cleveland?

Individuals in the staff and leadership benefited from the community organizing movement. It is much harder to assess whether the city of Cleveland really became more democratic because of the movement or if the legacies of the era live on in the collective capability of the neighborhoods to control their futures and meet challenges. While veterans of the era are emphatic about the positive impact of the movement on individual lives, they are more uncertain about the larger legacy.

Frank Ford of the Ohio Training Center felt that, for all the power that was developed, empowerment did not survive and neither did the democracy that came with it.[12] Kathy Jaksic of St. Clair Superior Coalition thought the question was hard to answer, but: "The activism did change the neighborhood. People were willing to bring up issues and concerns as they would never have before the coalition began."[13]

Tom Gannon agreed with Jaksic: "I think there is also a latent power sitting out there. I think someone could mobilize them." Marita Kavalec of Union Miles Community Coalition felt that it broadened the perspective of people in the neighborhoods to start to look at the city as a whole.[15]

It may be impossible to assess the contribution of the community organizing for the democratization of Cleveland during this period until the conservative lockdown of American politics and society ends. The lineages of activism, the way the ideas and experiences of America's insurgent traditions survive and develop are seldom noticed by the mainstream and are dismissed even by activists. The democratic legacy of this time probably will remain unclear until another period of activism takes the stage. Until then, the question remains unanswered.

The Great Failure

Veterans of the era are clear about where the community organizations failed. Sharon Bryant felt there was not enough development of skills of the individuals and activists of the groups. A failure of funding was also mentioned. However, the greatest failure of the community organizations is that few of the original groups still exist, creating a vacuum of advocacy work in Cleveland's neighborhoods that is felt to this very day. Marita Kavalec commented:

> Nobody took the responsibility to figure out where we were going. We had a number of well-developed, solid organizations with quality leadership and staff. We never made that a priority: Where do we go from here? That's the biggest problem with the movement and why it ended.[16]

Perhaps the greatest legacy of this era of activism in Cleveland is that it happened at all and that its values, issues and history is now part of the common heritage of all Clevelanders.

Chapter 11

NOTES FOR THE NEXT TIME

There is no such thing as society.
British Prime Minister Margaret Thatcher

I don't live in a desert. I live with other people.
Sarah Turner, *Buckeye Woodland Community Congress*

Activism did not die out after the period covered in this history. Significant campaigns have been launched, won, and lost since this.

The neighborhood based-activism that has continued since the mid-1980s, however, has been a pale shadow of its former self. Many attempts have been made to restore organizing to its previous glory. Many attempts are ongoing. None of these efforts has succeeded in seizing the public agenda and defining the debate on the future of the city and its neighborhoods as this period did.

Periods of activism cannot be willed into being. The most skilled organizers cannot change the direction of the winds of history. Even the founder of community organizing, Saul Alinsky, suffered through the doldrums of the early Cold War and the McCarthy era. It was not until the civil rights movement cracked the complacency and conformity of the Eisenhower era that space opened for his efforts to come to life. Alinsky's greatest days coincided with two of the most far-reaching eras of social change in American history, the 1930s and 1960s. The community organizing movement in Cleveland was no less dependent on the winds of American history. The movement could not have happened without the ferment and accomplishments of the social movements of the preceding decade.

The impact of the Reagan era's reaction cannot be underestimated. The entire focus of national life shifted from public to private. The primary goal of society was to get out of the way of the new American hero, the heroic entrepreneur.

Organizing today faces a much different world than it did in the early 1970s. The privatization of public services has provided public officials with a means to insulate themselves from blame when something goes wrong. The social safety net has been privatized through the use of nonprofit organizations. In many cases, this has propelled the society back to the pre-New Deal days when charity, not government programs, took care of society's forgotten. Meanwhile, the hyper-commercialization of American life has resulted in a society that looks less like a society and more like a continental theme park. Many corporations today make the average nation-state look like a third-rate fast food franchise. Where formerly it was possible to confront a bank or corporate leader who had a face and who lived in the community, that leader now may live in Atlanta, New York, London, or Singapore. In many cases, a community group would not be able to go to a hit in a van. They would have to obtain passports and airline tickets. If they found a CEO's house, it would be in a private gated community with armed security guaranteeing the CEO's privacy and peace.

The movement in Cleveland benefited from the persons it attracted. Organizers such as Tom Gannon, Karen Nielson, Joe Mariano and others, did not just come out of a training academy and become organizers as one would graduate from law school and pass the bar. Organizing, as Joe Garcia stated, was an art. It benefited from a cultural revolution that legitimized a lifelong commitment to social change. It takes such an alternative cultural refuge to sustain people in a society dominated by commercial values. As Harry Fagan commented, it has to be more than just a question of going into organizing or retailing. There has to be a passion that can come only from cultural movements working in tandem with powerful social movements.

We must be keenly aware of the cultural obstacles facing any project to revive organizing. The recent past and present have not been friendly toward creation of democratic cultures and movements. Through the 1980s and 1990s, the dominant culture returned to the American maxim that the business of America is business. This school of capitalism was dealt a blow by the dotcom bubble bursting and Wall Street scandals but it remains powerful in our society. Now an even more toxic environment has emerged from the smoke and ashes of the World Trade Center. The city on the hill has become a bunker.

We need to consider the peculiar cultural constraints to activism and democracy in Cleveland. Cleveland's population is composed of both international and domestic refugees who have fled fascism, communism, Jim Crow segregation, neo-colonialism in all its varieties, the "perfect dictatorship" of the Institutional Revolutionary Party (PRI) in Mexico, company towns, King Coal in Appalachia, and the autocracies of the Middle East. If we define democracy as the right to be left alone and the right to shop, these immigrants have found democracy in Cleveland. If we define democracy as participation in power, then their situation in Cleveland has only marginally improved.

The average Clevelander is born, lives out his or her life, and dies without experiencing one moment when his or her opinions or desires matter. Families, schools, and places of employment operate as miniature dictatorships. Voting is as foreign to most Clevelanders as books are to an illiterate household. Those who vote experience a brief, superficial contact with democracy. If they vote in every election, they will have experienced perhaps ninety minutes of democracy over their lifespan. The political culture of Cleveland is of little help to them because it is composed of ever-shifting proportions of paternalism, authoritarianism, and populism.

The organizing movement of the 1970s and 80s revolutionized how many individuals saw their lives and how they wanted to live their lives. Future movements must change the way entire communities look upon their collective lives and how they want to live in the future.

A renewed community organizing movement in Cleveland faces other issues beside its cultural milieu. Are the old Alinsky nostrums appropriate for the future? There are the issues of community organizing and politics, and the financing of community organizing, that need to be addressed.

Fundamentally we need to open up the entire field to experimentation and change. This process would revisit such questions as: What is community? What, if anything, do neighborhoods represent today? What is the relationship between neighborhoods and a downtown that is little more than an office/entertainment complex for suburbanites? What are the implications of the suburbanization of inner city neighborhoods with the arrival of McMansions, Big Box stores, and strip malls? Is an organizing philosophy developed in the ethnic neighborhoods of Depression-era Chicago still relevant? What is the purpose of organizing? To provide a cheering section for development projects, or something much deeper? Insurgencies and movements for change do not come from reading the manuals of the past. They arise when those manuals are read and discarded so that the activists and organizers of the future can write their own.

One flaw in the ideology of community organizing is the centrality of self-interest as a prime motivator for popular mobilizations. Self-interest organizing is attractive because it carries with it the aura of hardheaded pragmatism, a willingness to look at the world as it is and to act accordingly. This is a tonic for the disappointed idealist. Self-interest organizing also dovetails nicely into the rationale for capitalism: The way forward to a good society is for everyone to look out for number one.

The problem with self-interest organizing is that it is like the old tale of the blind men describing an elephant. It only describes part of what motivates individuals or communities to make the leap into activism.

Self-interest organizing has a long history of missed predictions. Prior to World War I, leaders of labor and socialist movements confidently predicted that the working classes of the industrial world would not go to war for the profits of their bosses. It was not in their self-interest. These leaders watched in horror as their working classes marched to the recruiting stations singing patriotic anthems as they went, and then slaughtered their fellow proletarians on the western front. The classic left never recovered from that shock.

The ideology of self-interest cannot explain a poor, unemployed factory worker who votes Republican because he is afraid of terrorists and doesn't want gays to marry. The ideology of self-interest has nothing to say about the importance of religious faith in the households of many Americans. The ideology of self-interest cannot explain the affluent leftist, or the dirt poor devotee of free-market dogma. The ideology of self-interest denies the importance of the varied and contradictory impulses that motivate our strange species. It is time to call into question the centrality of self-interest to community organizing theory. If self-interest is to have a future in that theory, it will have to be demoted to just one of many factors that motivate Americans to organize.

One motivation to organize is politics. We live in a world where one is either a participant in politics or the victim of those who do participate. Abstention is not a reasonable alternative for future efforts of community organizations. They cannot be credible in their declared mission of empowering the powerless while maintaining political chastity. This was the great tragedy of the Kucinich disaster, where natural allies failed to coalesce in a viable political coalition. Kucinich could have provided that political arm needed by the community organizations. It was not to be, but that does not mean that the issue is off the table.

The problems of involvement are obvious, but the consequences of participation are not nearly as severe as the consequences of not participating. Community organizations who abstain are the hostages of the prevailing political status quo.

How this could be implemented is only limited by the imagination. Community organizations could form political action committees. They would not need to join, but their leaders, staff, and rank and file could. They could found their own local party without depending on the political charity of the dominant parties. The very act of taking a political stance could aid in a process of self-definition. It would force organizations to ask tough questions: Who do we represent? What are we about? Who are our friends? Who are our foes? What is lacking in not the ability. It is imagination.

The next challenge is the linchpin, the challenge of funding community organizing. In Cleveland during the 1970s and 1980s, organizing was funded by foundation grants or by government programs such as VISTA. This was the Achilles' heel of the movement.

A constant question that hounds non-profit organizations is their degree of independence and, thus, their legitimacy in the face of outside funding. The much-heralded Third Sector may only be a colony of the powerful in the private and public sectors who use nonprofit organizations to hide or legitimize their agendas before the public.

Compounding this problem is the very nature of Alinsky-style organizing. It is expensive. Alinsky developed his ideas for organizing through involvement in the organizing of packing house workers in Chicago. They were funded through the

Congress of Industrial Organizations (CIO) and member dues. Who funds professional organizers for communities? In Chicago it was the Catholic Church, followed by philanthropists such as Marshall Fields, the heir to the department store fortune. This reliance on the church and philanthropists established a dependency on outside sources of funding. It is the fatal flaw in the idea of community organizing as it has developed since the 1930s.

A number of paths may solve or minimize this dilemma. The first is to rethink the entire architecture of organizing by developing forms that do not rely on expensive organizers running professional organizations.

The second solution is diversifying of funding sources to a mix of dues, internal fundraising projects, and foundation grants. The goal is to protect the organizations from having to turn off the lights and close up the office the moment one source of funding ends.

The third solution would be internal fundraising from dues. Community organizations could become true unions of community residents. Many balk at dues, saying communities would never support it. If this is true, it calls into question whether there is even a purpose to the groups, a purpose deemed important enough for the constituency to pay the price of having a community union.

A fourth alternative is for community organizations to seek a relationship with institutions that do have internal fundraising abilities. An alternative might be a relationship with the labor movement. Some veterans of the nonprofit world have even proposed that nonprofits form for-profit subsidiaries that could help fund the parent group. Again, the only resource in short supply is imagination.

Activism is the pulse of democracy. The future of community organizing is linked to the future of democracy. Since the founding of the republic, there has been an ebb and flow of democratic progress, a ceaseless, at times quiet and at times explosive, civil war between a democracy of wealth and a democracy of the people. Organizers must be willing to take the struggle for democracy into new venues without being trapped by the recipes, rhetoric, and strategies of the past. Social change, justice, and democracy have never had the upper hand, are seldom "practical" and are never where the smart money is bet. It is a hard road to travel, but we cannot forsake the dream of a democratic, just Cleveland. Community organizing's story in Cleveland is both history and prophecy, and the legacy of the movement of the 1970s continues to live on in Cleveland's people and their communities.

Notes

Chapter One - Cleveland: You Gotta Be Tough.

[1] Grabowski, John J. and Van Tassel, David D. The Encyclopedia of Cleveland History. Bloomington: Indiana University Press in association with Case Western Reserve University and the Western Reserve Historical Society, 1996, pages 566-568.

[2] Ibid., pages 972-975.

[3] Kusmer, Kenneth L. A Ghetto Takes Shape: Black Cleveland, 1870-1930. Urbana; London: University of Illinois Press. 1978, pages 67-90.

[4] Ibid., page 160.

[5] Moore, Leonard N., Carl B. Stokes and the Rise of Black Political Power. University of Illinois Press. Urbana   and Chicago. 2002, pages 47-51.

[6] Ibid., page 91-92.

[7] Encyclopedia of Cleveland History, pages 687-688.

[8] Swanstrom, Todd, The Crisis of Growth Politics: Cleveland, Kucinich and the Challenge of Urban Populism. Temple University Press. Philadelphia. 1985, page 214-215.

[9] Encyclopedia of Cleveland History, pages 445-447.

Chapter Two - See, Judge, Act.

[1] Fagan, Harry. *Empowerment: Skills of Parish Social Action*. Paulist Press, New York, 1979, page 8.

[2] Conway, Neil. Interview by author, June 5, 1994. Transcribed cassette recording. Randy J. Cunningham Community Organizing History Collection. Cleveland, Ohio: Western Reserve Historical Society archives.

[3] Gelm, Richard J. *Politics and Religious Authority: American Catholics Since the Second Vatican Council.* Westport, Conn.: Greenwood Press 1994, page 58.

[4] Begin, Rev. Bob, Interview by author, May 19, 1995. Transcribed cassette recording. Randy J. Cunningham Community Organizing History Collection. Cleveland, Ohio: Western Reserve Historical Society.

[5] Cleveland Catholic Peace Movement. Statement of April 10, 1968. Catholic Peace Movement papers. Cleveland, Ohio: Archives of the Diocese of Cleveland.

[6] Begin interview.

[7] Catholic Interracial Council of Cleveland. Board of Directors resolution of January 28, 1969. Catholic Peace Movement papers. Cleveland, Ohio: Archives of the Diocese of Cleveland.

[8] Presentation of Proposal for the Commission on Catholic Community Action, February 12, 1969. Commission on Catholic Community Action papers. Cleveland, Ohio: Archives of the Diocese of Cleveland.

[9] Ibid.

[10] Conway, Neil. Interview by author, June 5, 1994. Transcribed cassette recording. Randy J. Cunningham Community Organizing History Collection. Cleveland, Ohio: Western Reserve Historical Society archives.

[11] Reidy, Daniel F. Interview by author, March 21, 1996. Transcribed cassette recording. Randy J. Cunningham Community Organizing History Collection. Cleveland, Ohio: Western Reserve Historical Society archives.

[12] Ibid.

[13] Ibid.

[14] Ibid.

[15] Ibid.

[16] Conway interview.

[17] Gigante, Holly. Interview by author, February 15, 1994. Transcribed cassette recording. Randy J. Cunningham Community Organizing History Collection. Cleveland, Ohio: Western Reserve Historical Society archives.

[18] Murray, Charles. Interview by author, March 9, 1994. Transcribed cassette recording. Randy J. Cunningham Community Organizing History Collection. Cleveland, Ohio: Western Reserve Historical Society archives.

[19] Gigante interview.

[20] Paulo Freire and informal education. pages 1-2 in infed.org. www.infed.org/thinkers/et-freir.htm.

[21] Fagan, Harry. Interview by Earl Landau, February 17, 1983. Transcribed cassette recording. Randy J. Cunningham Community Organizing History Collection. Cleveland, Ohio: Western Reserve Historical Society archives.

Chapter Three - Establishing A Model

[1] Mariano, Joe. Interview by author, August 28, 1996. Transcribed cassette recording. Randy J. Cunningham Community Organizing History Collection. Cleveland, Ohio: Western Reserve Historical Society archives.

[2] O'Rourke, Lawrence M., *Geno: The Life and Mission of Geno Baroni*. New York: Paulist Press 1991, page 191.

[3] Reidy, Daniel Francis. *Urban Ethnic Organizing*. Ph.D. dissertation. University of Pittsburgh, 1972.

[4] Reidy interview.

[5] Reidy dissertation, 1972.

[6] Reidy dissertation, 1972.

[7] Evaluative Narrative. Project Interface. Campaign for Human Development (CHD) grant number 73-1234. Quarter I (November 1973 to January 1974). Buckeye Woodland Community Congress Collection. Cleveland, Ohio: Western Reserve Historical Society archives.

[8] Gannon, Tom to Reidy, Daniel F. Report for period February 12 to February 28, 1974. Project Interface. Buckeye Woodland Community Congress Collection. Cleveland, Ohio. Western Reserve Historical Society archives.

[9] Pertz, Barbara. Interview by author, March 27, 1994. Transcribed cassette recording. Randy J. Cunningham Community Organizing History Collection. Cleveland, Ohio: Western Reserve Historical Society archives.

[10] Ibid.

[11] Krumholz, Norman and Forester, John, *Making Equity Planning Work: Leadership in the Public Sector*. Philadelphia: Temple University Press 1990, page 137.

[12] Gannon, Tom. Interview by author, July 1, 1992. Transcribed cassette recording. Randy J. Cunningham Community Organizing History Collection. Cleveland, Ohio: Western Reserve Historical Society archives.

[13] *Making Equity Planning Work*, pages 139.

[14] Gannon interview.

[15] Mariano interview.

[16] Mariano interview.

[17] Mariano interview.

[18] Mariano interview.

[19] Kovach, Ken. Interview by author. April 2, 1994. Transcribed cassette recording. Randy J. Cunningham Community Organizing History Collection. Cleveland, Ohio: Western Reserve Historical Society archives.

[20] Gannon interview.

[21] Bryant, Sharon. Interview by author, June 24, 1992. Transcribed cassette recording. Randy J. Cunningham Community Organizing History Collection. Cleveland, Ohio: Western Reserve Historical Society archives.

[22] Barany, George. Interview by author, July 28, 1992. Transcribed cassette recording. Randy J Cunningham Community Organizing History Collection. Cleveland, Ohio: Western Reserve Historical Society archives.

[23] Killingsworth, Inez. Interview by author, September 26, 1992. Transcribed cassette recording. Randy J. Cunningham Community Organizing History Collection. Cleveland, Ohio: Western Reserve Historical Society archives.

[24] Barany interview.

[25] Kinney, Pat. Interview by author. May 4, 1994. Transcribed cassette recording. Randy J. Cunningham Community Organizing History Collection. Cleveland, Ohio: Western Reserve Historical Society archives.

Chapter Four - Building The Groups

[1] Doll, Henry. Interview by author, October 14, 1995. Transcribed cassette recording. Randy J. Cunningham Community Organizing History Collection. Cleveland, Ohio: Western Reserve Historical Society archives.

[2] Hudecek, Linda. Interviews by author, April 30 and July 16, 1992. Transcribed cassette recording. Randy J. Cunningham Community Organizing History Collection. Cleveland, Ohio Western Reserve Historical Society archives.

[3] Nielson, Karen. Interview by author, September 25, 1996. Transcribed cassette recording. Randy J. Cunningham Community Organizing History Collection. Cleveland, Ohio: Western Reserve Historical Society archives.

[4] Gruber, William Ondre. Interview by author, July 28, 1995. Transcribed cassette recording. Randy J. Cunningham Community Organizing History Collection. Cleveland, Ohio: Western Reserve Historical Society archives.

[5] Gruber personal papers.

[6] National Commission on Neighborhoods. *People, building neighborhoods: final report to the President and the Congress of the United States*. (Washington): The Commission. Superintendant of Documents, U.S. Government Printing Office, 1979. Case study appendix Vol. 1. Report on Citizens to Bring Broadway Back, pages 432-454.

[7] Gordeev, Denise. Interview by author, May 20, 1995. Transcribed cassette recording. Randy J. Cunningham Community Organizing History Collection. Cleveland, Ohio: Western Reserve Historical Society archives.

[8] Buccino, Paul. Interview by author, April 1, 1995. Transcribed cassette recording. Randy J.

Cunningham Community Organizing History Collection. Cleveland, Ohio: Western Reserve Historical Society archives.

[9] Kidd, Hugh. Interview by author, August 15, 1992. Transcribed cassette recording. Randy J. Cunningham Community Organizing History Collection. Cleveland, Ohio: Western Reserve Historical Society archives.

[10] Esposito, Ken. Interview by author, March 28, 1992. Transcribed cassette recording. Randy J. Cunningham Community Organizing History Collection. Cleveland, Ohio: Western Reserve Historical Society archives.

[11] Kavalec, Marita. Interview by author, May 9, 1995. Transcribed cassette recording. Randy J. Cunningham Community Organizing History Collection. Cleveland, Ohio: Western Reserve Historical Society archives.

[12] Wagner, Tom. Interview by author, June 29, 1996. Transcribed cassette recording. Randy J. Cunningham Community Organizing History Collection. Cleveland, Ohio: Western Reserve Historical Society archives.

[13] Ibid.

[14] Drury, Peggy. *Near West Neighbors In Action*. Cleveland, Ohio. July 1980. Near West Neighbors In Action Collection. Cleveland, Ohio: Western Reserve Historical Society archives.

[15] Mariano interview.

[16] Berry, Dan. Interview by author, September 19, 1995. Transcribed cassette recording. Randy J. Cunningham Community Organizing History Collection. Cleveland, Ohio: Western Reserve Historical Society archives.

[17] Training and Technical Assistance files. George Gund Foundation Collection. Cleveland, Ohio Western Reserve Historical Society archives.

[18] Ibid.

[19] Trapp, Shel. Interview by author, May 5, 2000. Cassette recording. Randy J. Cunningham Community Organizing History Collection. Cleveland, Ohio: Western Reserve Historical Society archives.

[20] Pratt, Ann. Interview by author, February 29, 1992. Transcribed cassette recording. Randy J. Cunningham Community Organizing History Collection. Cleveland, Ohio: Western Reserve Historical Society archives.

[21] Long, Gail. Interview by author. February 11, 1995. Cassette recording. Randy J. Cunningham Community Organizing History Collection. Cleveland, Ohio: Western Reserve Historical Society archives.

[22] Trapp interview.

[23] Barany interview.

[24] Reichtell, Bobbi. Interview by author, February 25, 1995. Transcribed cassette recording. Randy J. Cunningham Community Organizing History Collection. Cleveland, Ohio: Western Reserve Historical Society archives.

[25] Ibid.

[26] Kelly, Eileen. Interview by author, June 10, 1995. Transcribed cassette recording. Randy J. Cunningham Community Organizing History Interview collection. Cleveland, Ohio: Western Reserve Historical Society archives.

Chapter Five - Pols and Activists

[1] O'Brien, Michael. Interview by author, February 8, 1992. Transcribed cassette recording. Randy J. Cunningham Community Organizing History Collection. Cleveland, Ohio: Western Reserve Historical Society archives.

[2] Gannon interview.

[3] Weslian, Marlene. Interview by author, July 11, 1992. Transcribed cassette recording. Randy J. Cunningham Community Organizing History Collection. Cleveland, Ohio: Western Reserve Historical Society archives.

[4] Wagner interview.

[5] Kavalec interview.

[6] Pratt interview.

[7] Smith, Helen Knipe. Interview by author, February 19, 1996. Transcribed cassette recording. Randy J. Cunningham Community Organizing History Collection. Cleveland, Ohio: Western Reserve Historical Society archives.

[8] Ackerman, Chuck. Interview by author, January 6, 1996. Cassette recording. Randy J. Cunningham Community Organizing History Collection. Cleveland, Ohio: Western Reserve Historical Society archives.

[9] Kelly interview.

[10] *The Crisis of Growth Politics*, page 196.

[11] Ibid., page 196.

[12] Ibid., page 196.

[13] Barany interview.

[14] Hudecek interview.

[15] Buccino interview.

[16] Gannon interview.

[17] Buccino interview.

[18] Long, Karen D. "City Aides Bolt Conference on Neighborhoods." *The Plain Dealer*. November 5, 1978, section 1, page 1. Cleveland, Ohio: The Cleveland Public Library archives.

[19] Gannon interview.

[20] Gannon interview.

[21] Phipps, Peter and Swindell, Mary. "Weissman Strikes Back after Booing." *The Cleveland Press*. November 6, 1978, page A-1. Cleveland, Ohio: The Cleveland Public Library archives.

[22] Gruber personal papers.

[23] Kovach, Ron. "Nine on Board Quit St. Clair Coalition." *The Cleveland Press*. November 21, 1978, page D-4. Cleveland, Ohio: The Cleveland Public Library archives.

[24] Jaksic, Ron. Interview by author, September 2, 1995. Transcribed cassette recording. Randy J. Cunningham Community Organizing History Collection. Cleveland, Ohio: Western Reserve Historical Society archives.

[25] Ibid.

[26] Ibid.

[27] Grdina, Betty. "City Official Praises its Neighborhood Achievements." *The Plain Dealer*. May 26,

1979, page 25-A. Cleveland, Ohio: The Cleveland Public Library archives.

[28] Ibid.

[29] Ibid.

[30] Krumhansl, Bernice and Martin, Rev. Thomas. "The Coalition Speaks." *The Plain Dealer*. June 11, 1979, page 3-B. Cleveland, Ohio: The Cleveland Public Library archives.

[31] Jaksic, Ron interview.

[32] Murray interview.

[33] Barany interview.

[34] Gannon interview.

[35] Jaksic, Kathy. Interview by author, August 21, 1992. Transcribed cassette recording. Randy J. Cunningham Community Organizing History Collection. Cleveland, Ohio: Western Reserve Historical Society archives.

[36] Ford, Frank. Interview by author, December 30, 1992. Transcribed cassette recording. Randy J. Cunningham Community Organizing History Collection. Cleveland, Ohio: Western Reserve Historical Society archives.

[37] Gannon interview.

Chapter Six - The Battle Against Redlining

[1] Pertz, Barb. Interview by author, March 27, 1994. Transcribed cassette recording. Randy J.Cunningham Community Organizing History Collection. Cleveland, Ohio: Western Reserve Historical Society archives.

[2] Ibid.

[3] Reidy, Daniet F., *Greenlining: Reinvestment Strategies to Save Our Urban Housing*. Commission on Catholic Community Action. December 1974. Buckeye Woodland Community Congress Collection. Cleveland, Ohio: Western Reserve Historical Society archives.

[4] Ibid.

[5] Calkins, John. Interview by author, September 14, 1995. Transcribed cassette recording. Randy J. Cunningham Community Organizing History Collection. Cleveland, Ohio: Western Reserve Historical Society archives.

[6] O'Leary, Ruth Ann. *You Can Bet On It: Redlining in Cleveland*. The Commission on Catholic Community Action, 1974. Buckeye Woodland Community Congress Collection. Cleveland, Ohio: Western Reserve Historical Society archives.

[7] Calkins interview.

[8] Andrezjewski, Thomas S. "The $ Lever: West Siders Pledge to Withdraw Savings in Redlining Fight." *The Plain Dealer*. April 9, 1976. Page 7-C. The Cleveland Public Library archives.

[9] Garcia, Joe. Interview by author, April 15, 1995. Transcribed cassette recording. Randy J. Cunningham Community Organizing History Collection. Cleveland, Ohio: Western Reserve Historical Society archives.

[10] Ibid.

[11] Cogger, Janice, *The Impact of Foreclosures on Government Insured Mortgages in the Cleveland Area*. July 1977. The City of Cleveland Planning Commission. Cleveland, Ohio: Cleveland Public Library: Public Administration Library archives. Cleveland City Hall.

[12] Ibid.

[13] Hudecek (Mengay), Linda. *Disinvestment in the St. Clair Superior Community; Indications of Redlining*. March 1977. Class project, Cleveland State University. Personal papers of Linda Hudecek.

[14] Ibid.

[15] Ibid.

[16] *You Can Bet on It*.

[17] Nielson, Karen. Interview by author, September 25, 1996. Transcribed cassette recording. Randy J. Cunningham Community Organizing History Collection. Cleveland, Ohio: Western Reserve Historical Society archives.

[18] Ibid.

[19] Ibid.

[20] Ibid.

[21] Ibid.

[22] Kinney, Pat. Interview by author, May 4, 1994. Transcribed cassette recording. Randy J. Cunningham Community Organizing History Collection. Cleveland, Ohio: Western Reserve Historical Society archives.

[23] Kinney interview.

[24] Bryant, Sharon. Interview by author, June 24, 1994. Transcribed cassette recording. Randy J. Cunningham Community Organizing History Collection. Cleveland, Ohio: Western Reserve Historical Society archives.

[25] Jarrett, Jerry to M. Brock Weir. Memo of March 23, 1979. Buckeye Woodland Community Congress Collection. Cleveland, Ohio: Western Reserve Historical Society archives.

[26] Ibid.

[27] Ibid.

[28] Murphy, Michael J., "Fed board hears CleveTrust blasted." *The Plain Dealer*. August 23, 1979. Page 6-A. The Cleveland Public Library archives.

[29] Buckeye Woodland Community Congress to Federal Reserve Bank of Cleveland. Document of 12-12-79. Buckeye Woodland Community Congress Collection. Cleveland, Ohio: Western Reserve Historical Society archives.

[30] Ibid.

[31] Ibid.

[32] Ibid.

[33] Ibid.

[34] Ibid.

[35] Ibid.

[36] Ibid.

[37] Ibid.

[38] Bank Letter. "Fed to Ameritrust: Show You're Not Discriminating or Face Veto on Acquisitions." Vol. IV, No 2 January 14, 1980. Buckeye Woodland Community Congress Collection. Cleveland, Ohio: Western Reserve Historical Society archives.

[39] Bryant interview.

[40] Kinney interview.

Chapter Seven- Putting the Community into Community Development

[1] Aron, Gloria. Interview by author, March 21, 1992. Transcribed cassette recording. Randy J. Cunningham Organizing History Collection. Cleveland, Ohio: Western Reserve Historical Society archives.

[2] Mariano interview.

[3] Foster, Margaret. Testimony before Congress on community development reform. Buckeye Woodland Community Congress Collection. Cleveland, Ohio: Western Reserve Historical Society archives.

[4] Kovach, Ken. Letter to David O. Meeker, Assistant Secretary of the Dept. of Housing and Urban Development (HUD). August 28, 1976. Buckeye Woodland Community Congress Collection. Cleveland, Ohio: Western Reserve Historical Society archives.

[5] Andrezjewski, Thomas S. "Block grant gripes." *The Plain Dealer*. December 9, 1976, page 11-A. Cleveland, Ohio: Cleveland Public Library archives.

[6] The Cleveland Committee of the Citizens' Coalition for Block Grant Compliance. Working Draft: City of Cleveland's Grantee Performance Report 1976-77. A Preliminary Study. August 18, 1976. Cleveland, Ohio: Archives of the Diocese of Cleveland. Block Grant Compliance files.

[7] The Cleveland Committee of the Citizens' Coalition for Block Grant Compliance. Citizen Participation: Suggestions for Opening the Door for All Citizens. October 1976. Block Grant Compliance papers. Cleveland, Ohio: Archives of the Diocese of Cleveland.

[8] Star, Philip D. Chair of the Cleveland Committee. Letter to Ruth Miller – Director, Department of Community Development. May 11, 1977. Block Grant Compliance papers. Cleveland, Ohio: Archives of the Diocese of Cleveland.

[9] Ibid.

[10] Iskin, Peter M., Legal Aid Society of Cleveland. An Administrative Complaint. The Cleveland Committee of the Citizens' Coalition for Block Grant Compliance. July 27, 1977. Block Grant Compliance papers. Cleveland, Ohio: Archives of the Diocese of Cleveland.

[11] Ibid.

[12] "City, 5 Groups Settle Dispute Over Use of U.S. Funds. *The Plain Dealer*. July 7, 1978, page 5-A. Cleveland, Ohio: The Cleveland Public Library archives.

[13] Lombardi, Vince. Interview by author. June 30, 1999. Cassette recording. Randy J. Cunningham Community Organizing History Collection. Cleveland, Ohio: Western Reserve Historical Society archives.

[14] Clark, Gary R., "Block Grant Improvement Noted in Study Here." *The Plain Dealer*. September 1, 1981, page 8-A. Cleveland, Ohio: The Cleveland Public Library archives.

[15] Star, Phil. Interview by author, October 17, 2000. Cassette recording. Randy J. Cunningham Community Organizing History Collection. Cleveland, Ohio: Western Reserve Historical Society archives.

[16] Pollack, Bob. Interview by author, January 20, 1996. Transcribed cassette recording. Randy J. Cunningham Community Organizing History Collection. Cleveland, Ohio: Western Reserve Historical Society archives.

[17] Ibid.

[18] Aron interview.

[19] Ibid.

[20] Pollack interview.

[21] Aron interview.

Chapter Eight - Give us a Billion Dollars!

[1] Fagan, Harry. SOHIO campaign files. Buckeye Woodland Community Congress Collection. Cleveland, Ohio: Western Reserve Historical Society archives.

[2] Przbys, John J., "Elderly March; Plead for Fuel Cost Cut. October 13, 1979, page 6-A. *The Plain Dealer*. Cleveland, Ohio: The Cleveland Public Library archives.

[3] Kluk, Sandra. Interview by author, April 23, 1994. Transcribed cassette recording. Randy J. Cunningham Organizing History Collection. Cleveland, Ohio: Western Reserve Historical Society archives.

[4] Carney, Pat. Interview by author, June 19, 2000. Cassette recording. Randy J. Cunningham Community Organizing History Collection. Cleveland, Ohio: Western Reserve Historical Society archives.

[5] Lawless, James. "Many Beefs Spur Probe Into Bills of East Ohio Gas." April 11, 1980, page 3-B. *The Plain Dealer*. Cleveland, Ohio: The Cleveland Public Library archives.

[6] Callahan, Bill. Interview by author, February 4, 1995. Transcribed cassette recording. Randy J. Cunningham Community Organizing History Collection. Cleveland, Ohio: Western Reserve Historical Society, archives.

[7] Ibid.

[8] Trapp, Shel. Interview by author. May 5, 2000. Cassette recording. Randy J. Cunningham Community Organizing History Collection. Cleveland, Ohio: Western Reserve Historical Society archives.

[9] Callahan interview.

[10] Callahan interview.

[11] Curtiss, Pitt. Interview by author. September 28, 1995. Transcribed cassette recording. Personal collection of author.

[12] Kluk interview.

[13] Curtiss interview.

[14] Kluk interview.

[15] Curtiss interview.

[16] Callahan interview.

[17] Curtiss interview.

[18] Ibid.

[19] Ibid.

[20] Ibid.

[21] Fagan, Harry. Letter of May 6, 1982, to the Ohio Training Center and Neighborhood Directors. Buckeye Woodland Community Congress Collection. Cleveland, Ohio: Western Reserve Historical Society, archives.

[22] Ibid.

[23] Ibid.

[24] Ibid.

[25] Ibid.

[26] Trapp interview.

[27] Gannon, Tom. Letter of April 24, 1982, to Neighborhood People In Action (NPIA) Directors. Buckeye Woodland Community Congress Collection. Cleveland, Ohio: Western Reserve Historical Society, archives.

[28] Ibid.

[29] Ibid.

[30] Ibid.

[31] Barany, George. Letter of May 8, 1982 letter from Neighborhood People In Action to the public. Buckeye Woodland Community Congress Collection. Cleveland, Ohio: Western Reserve Historical Society archives.

[32] Ibid.

[33] Barany, George. Interview by author, June 24, 1992. Transcribed cassette recording. Randy J. Cunningham Community Organizing History Collection. Cleveland, Ohio: Western Reserve Historical Society archives.

[34] Fagan, Harry. Letter of June 3, 1982, to Ohio Training Center and staff and directors of community organizations. Buckeye Woodland Community Congress Collection. Cleveland, Ohio: Western Reserve Historical Society archives.

[35] Ibid.

[36] Ibid.

[37] Jaksic, Ron interview.

[38] Walker, Wesley. Interview by author, May 26, 2000. Cassette recording. Randy J. Cunningham Community Organizing History Collection. Cleveland, Ohio: Western Reserve Historical Society archives.

[39] Trapp interview.

[40] Kelly interview.

[41] Weslian, Marlene. Interview by author, July 1, 1992. Transcribed cassette recording. Randy J. Cunningham Community Organizing History Collection. Cleveland, Ohio: Western Reserve Historical Society archives.

[42] Ibid.

[43] Ibid.

[44] Kelly interview.

[45] O'Brien interview.

[46] Curtiss interview.

[47] Ibid.

[48] Ibid.

[49] Ibid.

[50] Ibid.

[51] Trapp interview.

[52] Esposito interview.

[53] Weslian interview.

54 Kelly interview.

55 Ibid.

Chapter Nine- The Movement Unravels

1 Fagan, Harry. Interview by Earl Landau, February 17, 1983. Transcribed cassette recording. Randy J. Cunningham Community Organizing History Collection. Cleveland, Ohio: Western Reserve Historical Society archives.

2 Gannon, Tom. Unrecorded conversation with author, 1999.

3 Ibid.

4 Calabrese, Len. Interview by author, April 1, 1996. Cassette recording. Randy J. Cunningham Community Organizing History Collection. Cleveland, Ohio: Western Reserve Historical Society archives.

5 Garcia interview.

6 Ibid.

7 Calabrese interview.

8 Doll interview.

9 Murray interview.

10 Wysocki, Ted. Letter to Sandra Kluk. April 21, 1981. Buckeye Woodland Community Congress Collection. Cleveland Ohio: Western Reserve Historical Society archives.

11 O'Rourke, Lawrence M. Geno: *The Life and Mission of Geno Baroni*. New York: Paulist Press 1991, page 166.

12 Training and Technical Assistance files. The George Gund Foundation Collection. Cleveland Ohio: Western Reserve Historical Society archives.

13 Doll interview.

14 Gannon interview.

15 Ibid.

16 Callahan interview.

17 Aron, Gloria and O'Brien, Michael interviews 1992.

18 Kavalec interview.

19 Pertz interview.

20 Zeller, George. Poverty Indicators – Cuyahoga County, Ohio. Volume 11 – 1994. Council for Economic Opportunities in Greater Cleveland, 1995.

21 Weslian interview.

22 O'Brien interview.

23 Ackerman, Chuck. Interview by author, January 6, 1995. Cassette recording. Randy J. Cunningham Community Organizing History Collection. Cleveland, Ohio: Western Reserve Historical Society archives.

24 Kluk interview.

25 Ibid.

26 Buckeye Woodland Community Congress. Executive Board minutes for June 21, 1984. Buckeye Woodland Community Congress Collection. Cleveland, Ohio: Western Reserve Historical Society archives.

[27] Bryant interview.

[28] Cooper, Alma. Interview by author, April 28, 2001. Cassette recording. Randy J. Cunningham Community Organizing History Collection. Cleveland, Ohio: Western Reserve Historical Society archives.

[29] Andrzejewski, Tom. "Buckeye Congress Backed Against Wall." *The Plain Dealer*. June 25, 1984, page 3-A. Cleveland, Ohio: Cleveland Public Library archives.

[30] Kovach interview.

[31] Tittle, Diana. *Rebuilding Cleveland: The Cleveland Foundation and Its Evolving Urban Strategy*. Columbus, Ohio: The Ohio State University Press, 1992, page 240.

[32] Andrezjewski, Tom. "Budget Cut to Tone Down Activism Here? *The Plain Dealer*. November 29, 1982, page 1-A. Cleveland, Ohio: Cleveland Public Library archives.

[33] Andrzejewski, Tom. "Cleveland's Neighborhood Leadership Is Slipping." *The Plain Dealer*. October 5, 1985, page 7-A. Cleveland, Ohio: The Cleveland Public Library archives.

Chapter Ten - Legacies

[1] Barany interview.
[2] Kelly interview.
[3] Killingsworth interview.
[4] Kidd, Hugh interview.
[5] Ford interview.
[6] Killingsworth interview.
[7] Kelly interview.
[8] Kavalec interview.
[9] Barany interview.

[10] Harrison, Norm. Interview by author, April 17, 1996. Transcribed cassette recording. Randy J. Cunningham Community Organizing History Collection. Cleveland, Ohio: Western Reserve Historical Society archives.

[11] Kavalec interview.
[12] Ford interview.
[13] Jaksic, Kathy interview.
[14] Gannon interview.
[15] Kavalec interview.
[16] Ibid.

Glossary

ACT   Active Clevelanders Together, primarily active on the west side in the mid- 1970s.

BETI   Buckeye Evaluation and Training Institute, was a training and technical assistance organization that advised neighborhood development corporations on such topics as weatherization and housing rehab. Based in the Buckeye neighborhood.

BOB   Bank on Buckeye, was a consortium of lenders organized to spur real estate and business investment in the Buckeye neighborhood.

BWCC   Buckeye Woodland Community Congress, active in the area of Buckeye and Woodland Avenues, south and west of Shaker Square.

CBBB   Citizens to Bring Broadway Back, which operated in the area adjoining Broadway Ave.

CCCA   Commission on Catholic Community Action, the social action arm of the Diocese of Cleveland and the primary sponsor of community organizing in Cleveland during the 1970s and 1980s.

CDBG   Community Development Block Grants, the primary source of federal community development funds for low- and moderate-income communities.

CHD   Campaign for Human Development, a Catholic social action foundation that helped fund much of the early organizing in Cleveland.

CHN   Cleveland Housing Network, a coalition of nonprofit housing development corporations founded in 1981.

CRA   Community Reinvestment Act. An act of Congress designed to prevent redlining by mandating that banks serve the credit needs of the communities in which they do business. The act allows community groups to challenge bank expansions or mergers if they feel they have not met the credit needs of their service areas.

FEMA   Federal Emergency Management Administration, a federal agency that funded many safety programs for neighborhoods.

HUD   Department of Housing and Urban Development.

LEAA   Law Enforcement Assistance Administration. Funded many neighbor-
             hood crime control programs until it was abolished by the Reagan
             administration.

OCBCA   Ohio City Block Club Association, community organization operating
             in the Near West Side/Ohio City neighborhood. Renamed Near West
             Neighbors in Action in 1979.

NPA   National People's Action, the national umbrella coalition of community
             organizations. Based in Chicago, it provided training, consultants, and
             a national network for the Cleveland organizations.

NPIA   Neighborhood People In Action, the name used by the Cleveland
             groups whenever they wished to act as a citywide coalition. In reality,
             it was a flag of convenience, rather than an actual organization.

NTIC   National Training and Information Center, the think tank, research,
             and policy arm of National People's Action and the agency that held
             the contract to train VISTAs in Cleveland.

NWNIA   Near West Neighbors In Action, the successor group to the Ohio City
             Block Club Association.

SCSC   St. Clair Superior Coalition, an organization active on the northeast
             side of Cleveland between St. Clair and Superior Avenues, east of
             downtown and west of Martin Luther King Jr. Blvd. Now known as
             the St. Clair Superior Neighborhood Development Association.

SOHIO   Standard Oil of Ohio, acquired by British Petroleum in the 1980s.

UMCC   Union Miles Community Coalition, an organization active on the
             southeast side of Cleveland. Merged with Union Miles Development
             Corporation (UMDC).

VISTA   Volunteers In Service to America, the domestic Peace Corps that paid
             for many of the block club organizers important to the Cleveland
             groups. It was downsized and its organizing mission was eliminated by
             the Reagan administration.

Bibliography

Fagan, Harry. *Empowerment: Skills of Parish Social Action*. New York: Paulist Press, 1979.

Grabowski, John J. and Van Tassel, David D. *The Encyclopedia of Cleveland History*. Bloomington: Indiana University Press in association with Case Western Reserve University and the Western Reserve Historical Society, 1996.

Gelm, Richard J. *Politics and Religious Authority: American Catholics Since the Second Vatican Council*. Westport, Conn.: Greenwood Press, 1994.

Krumholz, Norman and Forester, John. *Making Equity Planning Work: Leadership in the Public Sector.* Philadelphia: Temple University Press, 1990.

Kusmer, Kenneth L. *A Ghetto Takes Shape: Black Cleveland, 1870-1930*. Urbana; London: University of Illinois Press, 1978.

Moore, Leonard N. *Carl B. Stokes and the Rise of Black Political Power*. Urbana and Chicago: University of Illinois Press, 2002.

O'Rourke, Lawrence M. *Geno: The Life and Mission of Geno Baroni*. New York: Paulist Press, 1991.

Index

J

K

L

M

Democratizing Cleveland :

d